Language in use

INTERMEDIATE

Classroom Book

ADRIAN DOFF & CHRISTOPHER JONES

CAMBRIDGE
UNIVERSITY PRESS

PUBLISHED BY THE PRESS SYNDICATE OF THE UNIVERSITY OF CAMBRIDGE
The Pitt Building, Trumpington Street, Cambridge CB2 1RP, United Kingdom

CAMBRIDGE UNIVERSITY PRESS
The Edinburgh Building, Cambridge CB2 2RU, United Kingdom
40 West 20th Street, New York, NY 10011–4211, USA
10 Stamford Road, Oakleigh, Melbourne 3166, Australia

First published 1994
Sixth printing 1997

Printed in the United Kingdom at the University Press, Cambridge

ISBN 0 521 43552 8   Classroom Book
ISBN 0 521 43555 2   Self-study Workbook
ISBN 0 521 43554 4   Self-study Workbook with Answer Key
ISBN 0 521 43553 6   Teacher's Book
ISBN 0 521 43560 9   Class Cassette Set
ISBN 0 521 43561 7   Self-study Cassette Set

Split editions:
ISBN 0 521 43558 7   Classroom Book A
ISBN 0 521 43559 5   Classroom Book B
ISBN 0 521 43556 0   Self-study Workbook A with Answer Key
ISBN 0 521 43557 9   Self-study Workbook B with Answer Key
ISBN 0 521 43562 5   Self-study Cassette A
ISBN 0 521 43563 3   Self-study Cassette B

Contents

Guide to units

Classroom Book	Self-study Workbook

7 Past and present

Habitual actions in the past; describing changes; preparations

Grammar: used to; Past simple; Present perfect active and passive; not any more/longer

Grammar exercises
Listening: *Changed lives*
Pronunciation: *Syllables and stress*
Reading: *Two childhoods*

8 At your service

Vocabulary: having things done; using public services; evaluating services

Reading and listening activity: *Jobs we love to hate*

Vocabulary exercises
Listening: *On the phone*
Phrasal verbs: *Transitive verbs (1)*
Writing skills: *Punctuation: direct speech*

9 Imagining

Imagining things differently from the way they are; making wishes

Grammar: would; second conditionals; I wish + would / could / Past tense

Grammar exercises
Listening: *What would you do?*
Pronunciation: *Linking words: consonant + vowel*
Reading: *My perfect weekend*

10 Describing things

Vocabulary: describing objects by appearance and purpose; buying & selling

Reading and listening activity: *Great ideas?*

Vocabulary exercises
Listening: *Things for sale*
Phrasal verbs: *Transitive verbs (2)*
Writing skills: *Reference: this and which*

11 The future

Making predictions; hopes & expectations; giving reasons for predictions

Grammar: will/might; hope & expect; Future continuous; Future perfect; linking words

Grammar exercises
Listening: *When I'm 60 …*
Pronunciation: *Stress in sentences*
Reading: *Crossing the Sahara*

12 Accidents

Vocabulary: describing accidents and injuries; dealing with emergencies; road accidents

Reading and listening activity: *You're on your own*

Vocabulary exercises
Listening: *Narrow escapes*
Phrasal verbs: *Transitive verbs (3)*
Writing skills: *Joining ideas: clauses and phrases*

Review Units 7–12

Conversational English

1 *Making suggestions*
2 *Finding things in common*

Classroom Book	Self-study Workbook

13 Comparing and evaluating

Comparing things; comparing the way people do things; criticising and complaining

Grammar: comparative adjectives and adverbs; (not) as ... as ...; too & enough

Grammar exercises
Listening: *Living in Britain*
Pronunciation: *Linking words: consonant + consonant*
Reading: *Left-handedness*

14 The media

Vocabulary: newspapers and magazines, and their contents; types of TV programme
Reading and listening activity: *Easy listening*

Vocabulary exercises
Listening: *Media habits*
Phrasal verbs: *Double meanings*
Writing skills: *Similarities*

15 Recent events

Announcing news; giving and asking about details; talking about recent activities
Grammar: Present perfect simple active & passive; Past simple; Present perfect continuous

Grammar exercises
Listening: *What has happened?*
Pronunciation: *Changing stress*
Reading: *Personal letters*

16 Teaching and learning

Vocabulary: learning things at school; skills and abilities; education systems
Reading and listening activity: *Improve your memory*

Vocabulary exercises
Listening: *Three school subjects*
Phrasal verbs: *Prepositional verbs (1)*
Writing skills: *Letter writing*

17 Narration

Flashbacks in narration; changes in the past; reported speech and thought
Grammar: Past perfect tense; reported speech structures

Grammar exercises
Listening: *Locked in!*
Pronunciation: *Linking words with /w/ or /j/*
Reading: *Strange – but true?*

18 Breaking the law

Vocabulary: types of crime; types of punishment; courts and trials
Reading and listening activity: *Detective Shadow*

Vocabulary exercises
Listening: *A case of fraud*
Phrasal verbs: *Prepositional verbs (2)*
Writing skills: *Defining and non-defining relative clauses*

Review Units 13–18

Conversational English

1 *Giving advice*
2 *Making choices*

Classroom Book	Self-study Workbook

19 Up to now

Saying when things started; saying how long things have (or haven't) been going on

Grammar: Present perfect simple/continuous + for/since; negative duration structures

Grammar exercises
Listening: *Favourite things*
Pronunciation: *Stress and suffixes*
Reading: *Four logic puzzles*

20 In your lifetime

Vocabulary: birth, marriage and death; age groups; age and the law

Reading and listening activity: *A Good Boy, Griffith*

Vocabulary exercises
Listening: *Birth and marriage*
Phrasal verbs: *Three-word verbs (1)*
Writing skills: *Joining ideas: showing what's coming next*

21 Finding out

Asking for information; reporting questions; checking

Grammar: information questions; indirect questions; reported questions; question tags

Grammar exercises
Listening: *Phone conversation*
Pronunciation: *Changing tones*
Reading: *A bit of luck*

22 Speaking personally

Vocabulary: ways of describing feelings; positive & negative reactions

Reading and listening activity: *What's in a smile*

Vocabulary exercises
Listening: *James Bond films*
Phrasal verbs: *Three-word verbs (2)*
Writing skills: *Sequence: unexpected events*

23 The unreal past

Imagining what would have happened in different circumstances; expressing regret

Grammar: would have done; 2nd and 3rd conditionals; I wish + Past perfect; should(n't) have done

Grammar exercises
Listening: *A better place*
Pronunciation: *Common suffixes*
Reading: *If things had been different ...*

24 Life on Earth

Vocabulary: environmental problems and solutions; endangered species

Reading and listening activity: *The Doomsday Asteroid*

Vocabulary exercises
Listening: *How green are you?*
Phrasal verbs: *Review*
Writing skills: *Organising ideas*

Review Units 19–24

Conversational English

1 *Making offers*
2 *In the street*

Regular events

1 Personality types

Present simple tense

1 You want to find out what kind of person your partner is.
What other questions could you ask?

A culture-vulture

A sociable type

A home-lover

How often do you go to the theatre?
What kind of books do you read?
Do you ever go to art galleries?

Do you enjoy parties?

What do you do in the evenings?

An outdoor type

A workaholic

What sports do you do?

Do you work at weekends?

2 Interview your partner. What kind of person is he/she?

2 How often?

Twice a year if we can afford it.

About 20 a day.

Three times a day.

Every six months, but only for a check-up.

About once a week if there's anything good on.

About six cups a day.

1 What are these people talking about?
   What questions do you think they're answering?

2 Continue each of these remarks, using a frequency expression.

  a I like to keep in touch with my parents. I …
  b She loves hamburgers. She …
  c He's very religious. He …
  d That's one of our favourite restaurants. We …
  e He keeps himself incredibly clean. He …

3 National statistics

Present simple passive

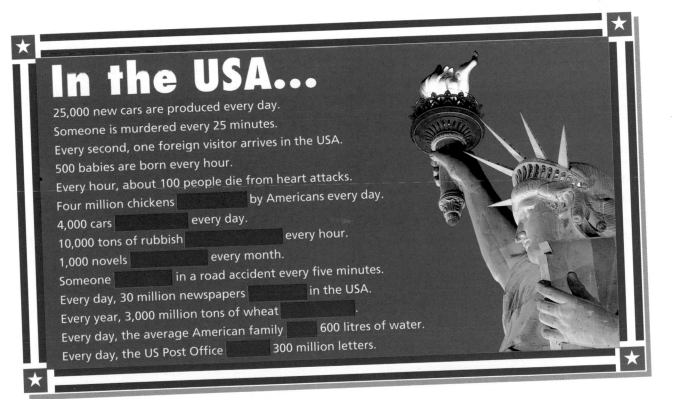

In the USA...

25,000 new cars are produced every day.
Someone is murdered every 25 minutes.
Every second, one foreign visitor arrives in the USA.
500 babies are born every hour.
Every hour, about 100 people die from heart attacks.
Four million chickens ▮▮▮ by Americans every day.
4,000 cars ▮▮▮ every day.
10,000 tons of rubbish ▮▮▮ every hour.
1,000 novels ▮▮▮ every month.
Someone ▮▮▮ in a road accident every five minutes.
Every day, 30 million newspapers ▮▮▮ in the USA.
Every year, 3,000 million tons of wheat ▮▮▮.
Every day, the average American family ▮▮▮ 600 litres of water.
Every day, the US Post Office ▮▮▮ 300 million letters.

1 Look at the first five statistics. Which verbs are active, and which are passive?

   Fill the gaps with active or passive forms of the verbs in the box.

publish	die	produce
sell	kill	grow
eat	throw away	deliver
steal	use	

2 Here are parts of other statistics about the USA. Can you complete them?

   2,500 bottles of Coca-Cola

   200,000 couples

   800,000 pairs of men's jeans

   51 kilos of red meat

   100,000 people visit Disney World

4 At the moment ...

1 You will hear five people talking about their jobs.

  a Here are some of the things they say.
    Match the remarks on the left with those on the right.
    What do you think the five jobs are?

  What do they do?

  I work for the *Daily Mirror*.
  I answer the phone.
  I spend a lot of time in libraries.
  I drive a tractor.
  I work for the United Nations.

  What are they doing at the moment?

  We're cutting down trees and mending fences.
  I'm covering the American elections.
  I'm doing some research on the First World War.
  We're building a dam in Ethiopia.
  I'm typing out our annual report.

  b 🔲 Now listen to the recording. What else does each person say?

2 Think of a job, and write two or three sentences saying
    – what you do in general
    – what you're doing at the moment.

    Read out your sentences one at a time, and see if your partner can guess your job.

Grammar Checklist

Present simple tense

Third person singular: add **-s** or **-es**
Negatives: **don't/doesn't** + *infinitive*
I **like** old films.
She **works** in Madrid.
I **don't like** old films.
She **doesn't work** in Madrid.

Present simple questions

(*Question word* +) **do/does** + *subject* +
infinitive
Do you **like** old films? (*not* ~~You like~~ ...?)
Where does she **work**? (*not* ~~Where she works~~?)
How often do you **go** to London?

Frequency expressions

I see them **twice a week**. (*not* ~~in a week~~)
He has milk **four times a day**.
I go to London **every three months**.
    (*not* ~~every third month~~)

Present simple passive

is/are + *past participle*
They grow coffee in Kenya.
→ Coffee **is grown** in Kenya.
Too many people **are killed** on the roads.
The magazine **is published** twice a year.

Present simple & continuous

Present simple – *for regular actions and talking 'in general'*.
Present continuous – *for activities 'around now'*.

She **works** for a marketing company, and she often **visits** the USA. Just now, she's **attending** a conference in Boston.
I **study** German literature. At the moment, I'm **writing** a paper on Goethe.

See also Reference section, page 130.

Focus on Form

1 Present simple

Look at the list and make guesses about your partner. Write complete sentences.

Example: *speak Russian*

She doesn't speak Russian.

a	speak Russian	e	take sugar in coffee
b	smoke	f	enjoy cooking
c	do crosswords	g	like chewing gum
d	like horror films	h	bite his/her fingernails

Your partner will tell you what he/she really does and doesn't do. See how many guesses you got right.

2 Present simple: questions

Student A: Look at Text 1 on page 112. Ask B questions to find out the missing information.

Student B: Look at Text 1 on page 114, and answer A's questions.

Example: The Tuareg live in ....

A Where do the Tuareg live?
B (They live) in the Sahara region of North Africa.

Now do the same with Text 2.

3 Frequency

Express the following ideas using frequency expressions.

Example: *at 9 a.m. and 9 p.m.*

(once) every 12 hours
twice a day

a on the 1st and 15th of every month
b on Monday, Wednesday and Friday
c in January, March, July and September
d at 9.00, 9.20, 9.40, 10.00 ...
e in 1985, 1987, 1989, 1991 ...
f at 7 a.m., 3 p.m. and 11 p.m.

Now make sentences using the expressions.

Example: I listen to the news twice a day.

4 The passive: processes

Look at the products in the pictures. Say what happens to them before they are used. Use the passive form of verbs in the box.

Example: *a packet of frozen peas*

First the peas are grown. Then they're picked ...

5 Simple or continuous?

Fill the gaps with the correct form of these verbs.

build	have	spend	work
enjoy	read	travel	write

a Mary .... a good rest in hospital, and I think she .... the change from her usual routine. Usually she .... so much time working that she (not) .... a chance to relax. Now she .... a lot of magazines, and .... letters to friends, and she says it's wonderful.

b Richard .... as an engineer for a large construction company. He .... six months of every year in Africa, where he .... from country to country supervising irrigation projects. At the moment, he's in Mali, where his company .... a dam.

6 Pronunciation

How do you say the words and phrases below?

a Do you go out a lot?
What kind of films do you like?
What does he do at the weekend?

b How often do you clean your teeth?
How often does she see her parents?

c cleaned   sold   produced   published
eaten   stolen   tasted   painted
The fish are cleaned.
The cars are painted.

Now listen and check your answers.

assemble	freeze
catch	grow
clean	paint
cook	pick
edit	print
write	wash
test	publish

Around the house

1 Easy to live with?

1 ▢ You will hear five people talking about the people they live with.

Listen and match what they say with the pictures.
How did the speakers use the words in the box?

mess	leave	tidy up
noise	put away	use up
clean	switch off	wash up

2 Are you an easy person to live with? Write a list of the things you do and don't do.

Now change lists with your partner. Do you think you could live in the same house or flat?

2 Labour-saving devices

1 Look at the labour-saving devices in the list.
What are they used for?
Add more items to the list.

Which do you think is the most useful?
Which is the least useful?

2 Think of an unusual labour-saving device
(either real or imaginary). Try to persuade
other students to buy it.

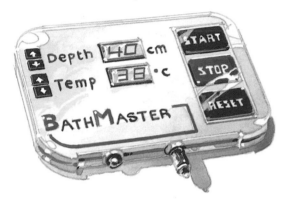

Device	Use
washing machine	Washing clothes
vacuum cleaner	
food processor	
fridge	
iron	—
dishwasher	
electric drill	

3 A place to relax

1 [cassette] You will hear someone imagining an
ideal room to relax in.

How similar is it to the room in the picture?

2 Imagine yourself relaxing in an ideal room.
– What are you doing?
– What's the room like? Think about the
things in the bubbles.

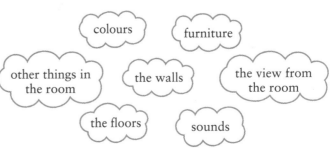

colours   furniture

other things in   the walls   the view from
the room   the room

the floors   sounds

4 Snow house

READING

1 Read the opening paragraph of the article *Inside the snow house*.

   Look at the writer's questions. What do you think the answers might be?

2 Now read the rest of the article.

   What were the answers to the writer's questions?

LISTENING

You will hear part of a TV programme in which someone builds an igloo.

1 🔲 The speaker demonstrates seven stages in building an igloo, but you will hear them in the wrong order. Listen and match what he says with the pictures.

2 🔲 Now listen to the whole description (in the right order) and write a sentence describing each of the stages 2–6.

Stage 1: Find an area of deep snow and mark out the shape of the igloo.

Stage 2:

Stage 3:

Stage 4:

Stage 5:

Stage 6:

Stage 7: The finished igloo.

Inside the snow house

Spending the winter in an igloo isn't as uncomfortable as you might think

Every five-year-old knows what igloos look like from the outside, but what are they like *inside*? And what would it be like to live in one? Imagine yourself inside a hollow dome made of snow and ice, with more ice underneath you. Would it be too cold to sit down comfortably? Would you be able to stand up, or would you have to crawl around on your hands and knees? And how would you keep warm? Could you light a fire? Wouldn't the fire fill the igloo with smoke and start melting the walls? The more you think about life in an igloo, the more problems there seem to be.

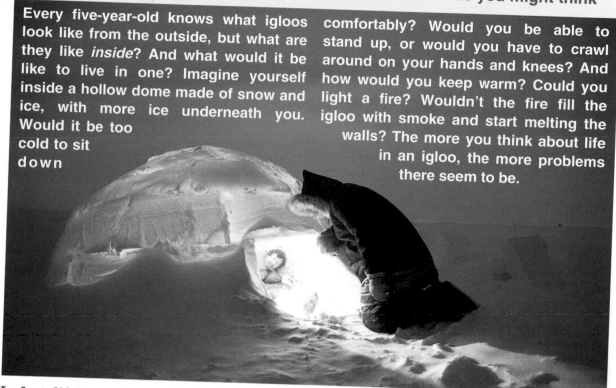

In fact, life in an igloo isn't nearly as uncomfortable as you might think. Let's imagine going into a traditional igloo out of a snowstorm in the middle of an Arctic winter ...

Room to move

The first thing you notice after crawling down through the entrance tunnel is that the igloo is bigger than it looks from the outside. The floor in the centre of the igloo is quite a bit below ground level, and there's plenty of room to stand up without banging your head.

Heat

It's also quite warm inside. This is partly because the snow blocks that the igloo is made from provide very good insulation, and partly because of a stone lamp burning seal oil – the only form of heating in the igloo. So although it's –30°C outside, it's a fairly comfortable +10°C inside – warm enough to take your wet clothes off and hang them up to dry.

Naturally, the heat melts a thin layer of the snow wall, but to prevent drips (and to provide even more insulation) there are animal skins hanging across the ceiling and down the walls.

It isn't smoky inside, either – a small hole in the ceiling acts as a chimney, and allows the smoke from the lamp to escape.

Light

Above the entrance tunnel, there's a thin sheet of ice set into the wall, which acts as a kind of window. You can't see much through it, but during the few hours of daylight it lets quite a lot of light in. The rest of the time, you can see by the light of the lamp (which is also used for cooking).

A place to sit

Around the walls of the igloo is a wide platform (which is at the same level as the ground outside), where you can sit or lie down. You don't have to sit directly on the snow – the platform is covered with dry grass and animal bones, then with animal skins, and finally with animal furs, and there are more animal furs to use as blankets. So the platform is a comfortable place to stretch out – and warm, too, as it is near the top of the dome where the warmest air is trapped.

A temporary home

In many ways, an igloo is the ideal place to spend a really cold winter. When the weather gets warmer in spring, of course, you no longer need it – which is just as well because that's the time that igloos start to melt.

3 Past events

1 Scary stories

Past simple & continuous tenses

She stopped the car and got out to have a look.

Mary was alone in the dark house.

Anna was driving along an empty forest road.

She sat up, frozen with fear.

Martha was walking home through the village square.

Suddenly she heard the sound of breaking glass downstairs.

She was lying in bed trying to get to sleep.

She saw a strange blue light flashing in the road ahead.

It was a stormy night, and the wind was howling through the trees outside.

As she was passing the church, the clock struck midnight.

A full moon was shining through the trees.

It was a dark and rainy night, and she was soaked to the skin.

Suddenly she heard a scream coming from the churchyard.

1 *a* Look at these sentences. Can you put them together to make the beginnings of three different stories?

   b Which parts of each story give the *background*, and which give the main *events*?

   c Imagine what happened next.

2 Work in groups. Choose one of the pictures, and write the beginning of a scary story.
   Think about these questions.
   – What time was it?
   – What was the weather like?
   – Where were the people?
   – What were they doing?
   – What did they see/hear/feel?
   – What happened?
   – How did they react?
   – What happened next?

2 Information gaps

Subject & object questions

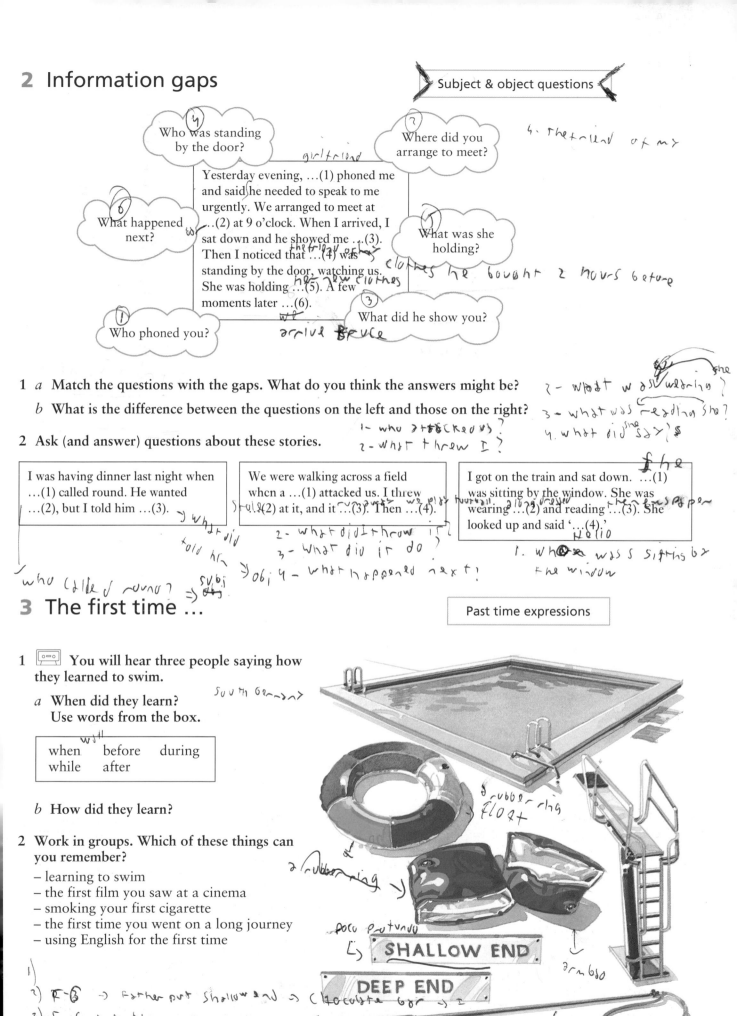

Who was standing by the door?

Where did you arrange to meet?

What happened next?

What was she holding?

Who phoned you?

What did he show you?

Yesterday evening, …(1) phoned me and said he needed to speak to me urgently. We arranged to meet at …(2) at 9 o'clock. When I arrived, I sat down and he showed me …(3). Then I noticed that …(4) was standing by the door, watching us. She was holding …(5). A few moments later …(6).

1 a Match the questions with the gaps. What do you think the answers might be?

b What is the difference between the questions on the left and those on the right?

2 Ask (and answer) questions about these stories.

I was having dinner last night when …(1) called round. He wanted …(2), but I told him …(3).

We were walking across a field when a …(1) attacked us. I threw …(2) at it, and it …(3). Then …(4).

I got on the train and sat down. …(1) was sitting by the window. She was wearing …(2) and reading …(3). She looked up and said '…(4).'

3 The first time …

Past time expressions

1 🔲 You will hear three people saying how they learned to swim.

a When did they learn?
Use words from the box.

when	before	during
while	after	

b How did they learn?

2 Work in groups. Which of these things can you remember?

– learning to swim
– the first film you saw at a cinema
– smoking your first cigarette
– the first time you went on a long journey
– using English for the first time

SHALLOW END

DEEP END

4 · many others destroyed / damaged
B - eventually they could rescue a few people
C- civilians killed during the night
d -

E - + police vehicle damaged too the when the
older

4 Bad news

Past simple passive

A The worst damage occurred in the city centre. Several of the older buildings collapsed and many others

B One village was completely cut off by the rising water, and many people were trapped in their houses for several hours. Eventually they

C The town came under heavy fire again last night as Government troops continued their advance. More than 100 civilians

D Passengers were thrown from their seats, and the driver, who was slightly injured,

E Police were attacked by crowds of youths throwing stones and home-made bombs. One police vehicle

1 *a* **Which of the newspaper articles is about**
   – a train crash?   – a riot?   – a war?
   – an earthquake?   – a flood?

  b **Which verbs in the articles are in the passive?**

   Complete the sentences in each article. Choose verbs from the box.

destroy	trap	rescue
damage	kill	overturn
injure	take	

2 **Choose one of the articles, and imagine what else happened. Write two or three sentences to continue the article.**

Grammar Checklist

Past simple tense

verb + -ed (or irregular forms) – for talking about events in the past.

They **elected** a new President.
I **heard** the news last night.

Irregular verbs: see list on page 143.

Past continuous tense

– for talking about the background to past events (what was going on at the time).

We **were** living in France at the time.
I heard the news while I **was** having breakfast.

Subject & object questions

*If **Wh-** questions are about the **subject** of the sentence, they keep normal word order.*

Who **invited** her to the party?
What **happened** next?
Who **was sitting** next to you?

Otherwise, they have question word order.

Who **did you invite** to the party?
When **did they arrive**?
What **were you doing**?
    (*Not* ~~What you were doing?~~)
Why **was he sitting** outside?

Past time expressions

We became friends **during** the war.

I met him | **when** / **while** | I was in Spain.

She worked there | **before** she went abroad. / **after** she left university.

Past simple passive

was/were + *past participle*
They **took** him to hospital.
→ He **was taken** to hospital.
The Chinese **invented** gunpowder.
→ Gunpowder **was invented** by the Chinese.

See also Reference section, page 131.

Focus on Form

1 Events and circumstances

Choose one of the events below and decide what was happening at the time. See if your partner can guess which event you are thinking of.

Examples:

A I was eating some lamb chops last night ...
B ... when I broke a tooth.

A While I was cycling through the park a few days ago ...
B ... a dog started chasing me.

My parents came home.
I tripped over.
All the lights went out.
A car nearly ran me over.
A dog started chasing me.
I broke a tooth.
Someone stole my wallet.
I fell asleep.
Someone shouted my name.

Now choose one of the situations you thought of and write one or two sentences saying what happened next.

2 Asking questions

Examples:

Alexander Fleming discovered penicillin in 1928.
Q Who discovered penicillin?

Columbus discovered America *in 1492*.
Q When did Columbus discover America?

Read your facts in the back of the book and ask your partner questions.

Student A: Your facts are on page 112.
Student B: Your facts are on page 114.

3 Saying when things happened

Imagine when these things happened. Complete the sentences, using *when*, *while*, *before*, *after* or *during*.

Example: *They decided to get divorced ...*

... during their honeymoon.
... after they had their fourth child.
... when they both fell in love with other people.

a He broke his arm ...
b It was so embarrassing! I fell asleep ...
c She found it difficult to get a job ...
d I had plenty of time to read ...
e I forgot to renew my passport ...

4 Past simple passive

Example:

A He didn't die of a heart attack.
B He was murdered.

Student A: Read out the sentences below.

Student B: Choose suitable continuations from the box, and change them into the passive.

a He didn't die of a heart attack.
b I didn't lose my credit cards.
c She doesn't work there any more.
d He didn't fall out of the window.
e I've got my brief-case back.
f His parents died when he was three.
g We didn't go to the party.
h Actually, it's not a Picasso.

His grandmother brought him up.
Someone pushed him.
Someone stole them.
My daughter painted it.
Someone found it on a bus.
They didn't invite us.
Someone murdered him.
They sacked her last week.

5 Pronunciation

How do you say the words and phrases below?

a He was sitting next to me.
They were watching television.
What were they watching?

b Did you know?
Why did she phone you?
What did she say to you?

c destroyed damaged injured
rescued murdered
He was murdered.
Several buildings were damaged.

Now listen and check your answers.

1 You and your money

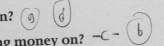

1 Do you spend more than you earn?
2 What do you most enjoy spending money on?
3 What do you least enjoy spending money on?
4 What do you think is good value for money?
5 What do you think is a waste of money?

6 What can you afford that you most appreciate?
7 What can't you afford that you would most like to have?

a Life insurance — I'm not planning to die just yet. And expensive haircuts.

a Potatoes, rice, pasta, things like that. They're cheap, and they fill you up!

b I like being able to buy good quality food and clothes, and not having to look around to find the cheapest of everything.

b A plane ticket, when I can afford it. That gives me a really great feeling.

c A really nice, old, classic car. My first choice would be a Jaguar XK150.

c Oh, lots of things — fur coats, caviare, designer shoes and unnecessary make-up, for example. And tobacco.

d No, but I don't save anything either.

d This stupid Government tax. I don't think students should pay taxes.

e Take-away restaurants which take your order over the phone and deliver the food right to your door — free.

e A round-the-world plane ticket, with lots of stopovers in nice places.
A car plus enough money to keep it running.

f Boring things like suits and white shirts and ties to wear to work. And buying train tickets every day to get to work and back.

f Yes. I have to borrow from my parents, and also from a student loan company.

g A really good night out at the weekend. Or preferably two.

g I'm pretty lucky to have enough money to study, and to do a bit of travelling.

1 Here are the answers two people gave to the questions at the top of the page.

   Can you match their answers to the questions?
   What can you tell about each of the people?

2 Spend some time thinking of your own answers to the questions.

   Now work with a partner. Interview each other.

2 Exchanges

Can you give me change for a £10 note?

I can pay you back on Friday.

Can I just buy some chewing gum, please?

Did you bring your receipt with you?

Do you think you could lend me £20?

I'd like to pay my bill, please.

You'll need to sign them just here, please.

Do you take credit cards?

I'd like to cash some traveller's cheques.

I'd like a refund, please.

1 🔲 You will hear five short conversations about money. Look at the remarks in bubbles. Which two remarks do you think you will hear in each conversation?

Now listen to the recording, and see if you were right.

2 Work in pairs. Choose one of the remarks and develop it into a conversation of your own.

3 The cost of living

1 Think of an average family in your country. What are the main expenses they have to pay?

2 Read this election manifesto. What do you think the name of the party is?

The ▮▮▮▮▮▮ Party

ELECTION MANIFESTO

1 We will spend more money on roads and motorways.

2 We will spend less money on public transport.

3 We will reduce the price of petrol.

4 We will abolish car tax.

5 We will halve the price of car insurance and driving lessons.

6 We will provide free parking in all city centres.

In groups, form your own political party.

– What is your party called? What is its aim?
– Write your election manifesto.

4 Can you make a million?

READING

This is a reading game in which your aim is to make £1,000,000.

Start at Card 1, and decide what you want to do. Then turn to the card indicated by your choice. For example, if you decide to go to university, go on to Card 12, which is on page 114.

Each card represents at least two years of your life.

As you play, make notes in the table below. The game ends either when you reach 36 years of age or when you have £1,000,000.

> **1** You're 18, and it's time to leave school and decide what to do with your life. Your best subjects were maths and economics, but you are also interested in art and graphic design.
>
> Your parents would like you to study economics at university for four years, and then follow a career in the Civil Service. Or you could go to design college for two years, and then go into advertising. A third possibility would be to get a job in a bank, where you can use your maths and start earning money straight away.
>
> Your savings at the moment total £5,000.
>
> Go to university ➤ **12** (p.114)
> Go to design college ➤ **10** (p.113)
> Join a bank ➤ **18** (p.115)

Age	Card no.	Place	Occupation	Money
18	1	Home	Leaving school	£5,000
18–20				
20–22				
22–24				
24–26				
26–28				
28–30				
30–32				
32–34				
34–36				

LISTENING

You will hear parts of an interview with someone who made £1,000,000. Listen to each part and follow his career, starting with Card 1.

Part 1
– Which card is he on now?
– What do you think he'll do next?

Part 2
– Which card is he on now?
– What do you think he'll do next?

Part 3
– Which card is he on now?
– What finally made him a millionaire?

2 Congratulations! You got your degree in economics. You can now get a well-paid job in the Civil Service, with good chances of promotion – this is what your parents would like you to do.

Or you could drop everything and go to Brazil – a friend of yours is working there and says she could probably find you a job.

You didn't spend much in the last two years at university – you have £1,000 less than you did two years ago.

Join the Civil Service ➤ **11** (p.113)
Go to Brazil ➤ **14** (p.114)

3 You're enjoying life – you and your friend work well together, you're living in a nice part of the country, and you've made a lot of new friends.

Designing toys is hard work – there seem to be so many already on the market – and it's taking you time to build up contacts. In your first two years you made a slight *loss* – nothing to worry about, but you now have £15,000 less money than two years ago.

You *could* get a nice safe job with a firm of accountants, but on the other hand, perhaps the toy business will take off …

Stay in the toy business ➤ **15** (p.114)
Join a firm of accountants ➤ **24** (p.116)

J&B DESIGN STUDIO

4 After two years in the Caribbean as a crew member of the yacht *Passing Clouds*, you've begun to suspect that something illegal is going on. You've often seen your passengers talking in whispers and exchanging mysterious packages – and isn't £30,000 a year a bit *too* much for the job you're doing?

You could leave the ship now and go back home (your father says there's a job in the Civil Service still open for you) – or take a risk and carry on working on *Passing Clouds*. You've added £50,000 to your savings over the last two years.

Stay in the Caribbean ➤ **23** (p.116)
Join the Civil Service ➤ **16** (p.115)

5 You've had a good two years. You were promoted twice and you're now earning a good salary – with plenty left over to invest. You invested money at the right time, too – share prices doubled over the last year, and altogether you now have 50% more than you had two years ago.

But you're bored – you could carry on in the Civil Service, or you could just drop everything and go off on a trip round the world … you never know what might happen to you.

Stay in the Civil Service ➤ **13** (p.114)
Go round the world ➤ **17** (p.115)

5 Obligation

1 Overseas experience

Obligation structures

1 *a* Look at this advertisement. What other questions might you ask?

Do I have to pay tax?

Do I have to pay my own fare?

Do I need a work permit?

Can we go away at weekends?

Are we allowed to use the hotel's facilities?

Do I have to ...?

...?

Can I ...?

Work abroad this summer
in an Interplex international hotel

✔ No formal qualifications needed

✔ Varied and interesting work

✔ Free accommodation

✔ Earn money and see a foreign country

b Now read the information sheet on page 112. What are the answers?
Talk about things you

– can / are allowed to do
– can't / aren't allowed to do
– have to / need to do
– don't have to / don't need to do.

2 Choose one of these advertisements.

Student A: You're interested in finding out more. Think of some
questions. Then find out the answers from B.

Student B: You represent the company that placed the advertisement.
Think of the information you will give. Then answer A's questions.

Au pairs needed for European families

Learn a foreign language in the country of your choice. Full board and pocket money given in return for child care and light housework.

Learn English in Britain this summer

● 4-week residential courses in beautiful countryside
● Fully qualified teachers
● Friendly accommodation with local families.

Why not work on a farm this summer?

Fresh air, good food, lots of exercise: what better way of spending the summer? And you'll be earning money instead of spending it!

2 Strict or easy-going?

make & let

1 What's the difference between the teachers of these two students? Talk about each one using *make* and *let*.

Imagine other things that the two teachers do and don't do.

We're allowed to wear what we like in class.

We don't have to do much work.

We're not allowed to talk in class.

We have to do loads of homework.

2 Choose one of the pictures and write a sentence about them using *make* or *let*. See if other students can guess who you chose.

Strict parents

A strict dog-owner

A strict boss

A strict government

Easy-going parents

An easy-going dog-owner

An easy-going boss

An easy-going government

3 Punishments

Past obligation structures

1   You will hear three people talking about punishments they received when they were at school. For each one, say
– what they did wrong
– what the punishment was.

Do you think the punishments were fair?

2 Work in groups. Tell the others about something you had to do (or weren't allowed to do) as a punishment.

Choose the most interesting punishment and tell the rest of the class about it.

4 Feel free

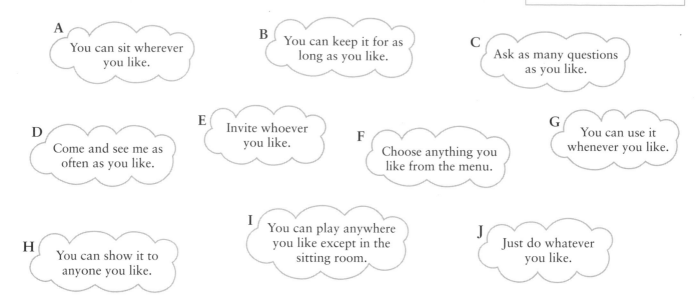

A You can sit wherever you like.

B You can keep it for as long as you like.

C Ask as many questions as you like.

D Come and see me as often as you like.

E Invite whoever you like.

F Choose anything you like from the menu.

G You can use it whenever you like.

H You can show it to anyone you like.

I You can play anywhere you like except in the sitting room.

J Just do whatever you like.

1 Look at the remarks in bubbles. Make a list of
  – words like *wherever*
  – words like *anywhere*
  – expressions with *as ... as*.

2 Imagine you're staying with a friend who's very easy-going.
  How might he/she answer these questions?

  – Where shall I put my coat?
  – Can I watch the news on TV?
  – Can I have one of these apples?
  – What time shall I get up?
  – Can I phone my sister?

  Now continue with questions of your own.

Grammar Checklist

Obligation

(don't) have to; (don't) need to

You **have to** show your passport at the border.
You **don't have to** wear a tie.
We **don't need to** be there till 7 o'clock.

Do I have to show my passport?
Do we need to buy tickets?

Permission

can('t); are(n't) allowed to

Sorry – you **can't** smoke in here.
She's **allowed to** have visitors.

Can I smoke in here?
Is she **allowed to** have visitors?

make & let

make & **let** *are followed by infinitive <u>without</u>* to.

Her parents **make** her **tidy** her own room.
   (= she has to tidy it)
They **don't make** her **cook** her own meals.
   (= she doesn't have to cook her own meals)
They **let** her **stay** up late at weekends.
   (= she's allowed to stay up late)
They **didn't let** me **use** the phone.
   (= I couldn't use it)

Freedom from obligation

| You can ask | **whoever** / **anyone** | you like. |

| You can sit | **wherever** / **anywhere** | you like. |

You can eat **as much as you like.**
They can stay **as long as they like.**

See also Reference section, page 132.

Focus on Form

1 The law: obligation structures

Change these sentences (if necessary) so that they are true of your country.

a Passengers in cars don't have to to wear seat-belts.
b You're not allowed to drive faster than 100 kph.
c You don't have to pay for local phone calls.
d Everyone has to carry an identity card.
e Foreigners can't own land and property.
f Men and women have to retire at 65.
g You're allowed to smoke on buses and trains.
h Men and women have to do two years' military service.

2 Make & let

Student A: **Choose an item from Box A, and make a positive or negative sentence with** *let*.

Student B: **Choose an item from Box B, and make a sentence with** *make*. **Your sentence should mean the same as A's.**

Examples:

A His parents don't let him stay up late.
B They make him go to bed early.

A My dad let me stay up late last night.
B He didn't make me go to bed early.

Box A:
let

stay up late
use our own language in class
have the day off
wear jeans
sleep on the bed
go straight in
pay by credit card
stay the night

Box B:
make

pay in cash
wait in the queue
go home
come into work
wear a suit
sleep in a basket in the kitchen
go to bed early
speak English all the time

3 Past obligation

Student A: **Choose a sentence from the box, and imagine what happened beforehand.**

Student B: **Can you guess what happened next? Choose one of the sentences in the box.**

Example:
A Last night we went to the cinema, and it finished so late that we missed the last bus …
B … so we had to walk home.

… we had to walk home.
… we didn't have to buy one.
… they made us wait till the interval.
… they finally let us go home.
… we couldn't get out.
… we let them stay with us.
… we didn't have to cook.
… we had to leave a note.

4 Do whatever you like

Change these sentences so that they end in … *you like*, … *she likes*, **etc.**

Examples:

She's allowed to eat crisps, sweets, ice-cream …
She's allowed to eat whatever she likes.

You can sleep for 8 hours, 9 hours, 10 hours …
You can sleep as long as you like.

a His parents let him watch cartoons, westerns, soap operas …
b We can have lunch at 12.00, 1.00, 2.00 …
c She can borrow one book, two books, three books …
d I'll take you to the museum, to the zoo, to the park …
e You can drive at 90 kph, 120 kph, 150 kph …
f You can phone Ken, Laura, Stephen …
g They can have £100, £200, £300 …

5 Pronunciation

How do you say the words and phrases below?

a I have to stay here.
   Do you have to do homework?
   Do we need to pay?
   We're allowed to go out.
   You aren't allowed to look at it.

b She made them work.
   He let them stay up.

c wherever   whoever   however
   You can sit wherever you like.
   They can stay as long as they like.

⌷ **Now listen and check your answers.**

6

On holiday

1 Away from it all

St. George's

Gren...

On Tuesday morning we arrived at the port of St. George's, Grenada's capital city. Most people decided to join the [____] round the island, which included a [____] to a spice plantation and Carib's Leap, the cliffs where, in the 17th century, the last of the Carib Indians are said to have jumped to their death rather than become slaves. Some of the group, including myself, preferred to look around St. George's itself. We spent a fascinating morning in the [____], where you could buy all kinds of [____] produce: fruit, spices, straw hats and rugs (popular as [____]) and a bewildering variety of fish. For lunch, we ate crab soup and turtle steaks (both local [____]), and drank rum punch, which was a bit strong for my taste. Later on, we went [____]: we saw the cathedral, the 18th century Fort Rupert (now the headquarters of the Grenada police force) and, surprisingly, a zoo, before rejoining the rest of the party for an early evening barbecue on a sandy [____] a few kilometres along the [____]. Then a last stroll along the harbour, and back to the ship.

1 Here is part of a travel article. Fill the gaps with words from the box.

souvenirs	market	coast
specialities	visit	local
sightseeing	excursion	beach

Now look at these pictures. Make a list of activities for each type of holiday.

2 You are either a *travel agent* or a *tourist*.

Travel agents: Think of a holiday destination and decide what you will say about it. Then visit each group of tourists in turn.

Tourists: Decide what you want to know about each place. Then listen to each travel agent and ask any questions you have.

Which holiday destination will you choose?

2 Packing list

1 Look at the packing list. Where do you think the person is going?

two jumpers
map
water bottle
anorak
matches
tent
binoculars
insect repellent
sleeping bag

2 Choose a holiday destination and imagine what kind of holiday it might be.

Make a list of 10 things you would take with you. Use a dictionary to help you.

Other students will guess where you're going.

3 Festival

1 [cassette] You will hear someone talking about the origin of the Chinese Dragon Boat Festival. What does the speaker say about

– Chow Yen?   – drums?
– boats?   – dumplings?

[cassette] Now listen to her describing what happens in the Festival. What do people do with boats, drums and dumplings now?

2 Work in groups. Choose a festival in your own country.

What do you know about it?
What aren't you sure of?

Write questions to ask other students.

4 Culture shock

1

[handwritten: British Singapore]

- Don't be surprised if people you don't know well ask you how much you earn or how much your car cost. This is quite normal.
- If you are invited for a meal, people will always offer you a second helping. You should always say 'No', so as not to appear greedy. This will be understood, and your host will give you more anyway. If you really don't want any more, cover your plate with your hand.
- It is polite to leave some food on your plate at the end of a meal – if you eat everything, it's a sign that you want more.
- Don't drop litter – even cigarette ends. It will be noticed, and you'll be fined. You can also be fined if you fail to flush the toilet in a restaurant or other public place.
- In general, it is considered insulting to give tips, and many places have signs saying 'No tipping'.

2

[handwritten: West Africa]

- Greetings can go on for some time – 'How are you? How is the day? How's business? How's the family?' … Your answer should always be 'Fine', even if you're not. If there's a gap in the conversation, this is usually filled with more greetings.
- Holding hands is common, even between strangers. Don't be surprised if someone showing you the way down the street leads you by the hand.
- In general, the left hand is used for 'unclean' activities, so use the right hand for giving things to people, handling food, etc.
- People younger than you will avoid looking you straight in the eye. This is not rude – on the contrary, it is a sign of respect.
- Hissing is a common way of attracting a person's attention, and is not rude. It's quite normal to hiss to call a waiter to your table.

READING

1 Here are some texts containing tips for visitors to five different parts of the world. Which text do you think is about

- – Britain?
- – Spain?
- – Singapore?
- – Thailand?
- – West Africa?

Which tips are illustrated in the pictures?

2 According to the texts, where is it either *polite* or *impolite* to

- *a* leave food on your plate?
- *b* visit someone without an invitation?
- *c* touch food with your left hand?
- *d* ask someone how much they earn?
- *e* look your boss straight in the eye?
- *f* open a present immediately?
- *g* arrive on time?

3 Imagine yourself in one of the five places. Which customs would you find it

- – easy to get used to?
- – difficult to get used to?

4 Imagine that someone from one of the five places is coming to visit you.

What tips would you give them about your own country?

A

LISTENING

You will hear someone talking about something that happened to him in the Sudan. The story is in three parts.

Part 1
- What was he doing?
- How many people were there?
- What did they start doing?
- What do you think the speaker did next?

Part 2
- What did everyone eat?
- Why do you think they didn't eat the tomatoes?

Part 3
- Why didn't they eat the tomatoes?

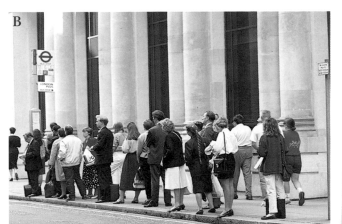

B

3

- People regard their homes as very private places, so if you're asked out to a meal it'll probably be to a restaurant rather than to the person's house or flat.
- It's common to see young children eating in restaurants with their parents, even quite late at night.
- Evening activity starts late. Restaurants start to fill up around 10 o'clock, and nightlife can carry on till four or five in the morning – or even later.
- Kissing (on both cheeks) is a common form of greeting between women, and between women and men. It is unusual between men, except when greeting a member of the family or a close friend.
- If it's your birthday, you're expected to invite friends or colleagues for a drink or a meal. You're the host, so you're expected to pay.

C

D

4

- Kissing is not common as a form of greeting unless you know someone well. It is especially unusual between men, who usually shake hands or just say 'Hello' without touching. People usually kiss on one cheek only.
- Unless you know someone well, it's impolite to ask them how much they earn, or how much they paid for something.
- In shops and at bus stops, go to the back of the queue and wait. If you 'jump the queue', other people will angrily tell you to wait your turn.
- Punctuality is important. If you arrange to meet someone, try not to be more than a few minutes late.
- On trains, especially underground trains, people tend to sit in silence and read. If you try to start a conversation with the person next to you, don't be surprised if you don't get much of a response.

5

- The head is considered the most spiritual part of the body, and the feet the dirtiest part, and it is very impolite to point your foot at someone, especially at their head. So don't sit with one leg crossed over the other, and never put your feet up on a chair or a desk.
- It is also rude to point at people with your finger. If you must point at someone, do it by nodding your head. If you want to call a waiter, do it with your palm down, moving your fingers towards you.
- It's quite normal to visit people at home without being invited. If you do, take a small gift with you.
- If you give someone a gift, they will usually thank you for it and put it aside without opening it. Don't be offended – it's bad manners to open a present in front of the person who has given it.

Adapted from *Britain, Singapore, Spain, Thailand* in the *Culture Shock* series; *The Rough Guide to West Africa*.

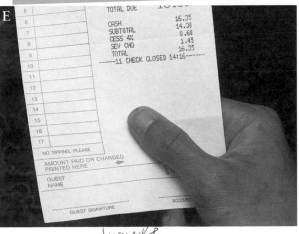

E

Review: Units 1–6

Find out

1 Find out how often other students do these things.
- – drink coffee
- – wash up
- – go on holiday
- – go to the bank

2 A Think of someone interesting that you know. What's his/her name?
Other students: Find out what the person does, and what they're doing at the moment.

3 A Ask questions to find out as much as you can about what B did last weekend.
B Answer A's questions, but don't give any information that he/she doesn't ask for.

Role-play

1 A You've seen an advertisement for a room to let. Ring up and find out what it's like.
B A is interested in renting a room from you. Tell him/her what it's like.

2 A You're at an exchange office. You want to change some US dollars, and change some traveller's cheques. Make sure you get a receipt.
B Serve the customer. Don't forget to ask for his/her passport.

3 A You're visiting a friend in prison. Find out what some of the rules are.
B Tell your friend what you have to do and what you are(n't) allowed to do.

Conversational English

1 Making requests

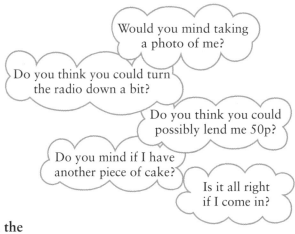

1 Compare the requests on the left and those on the right. Why do you think the second speaker is asking more carefully?

2 Make suitable requests for one of these situations.
- – You're in hospital. Think of some things to ask the nurse.
- – You're staying at a hotel. Think of some things to ask the receptionist.
- – You're on a bus. Think of some things to ask the person next to you.

Now think of some real requests to ask your partner.

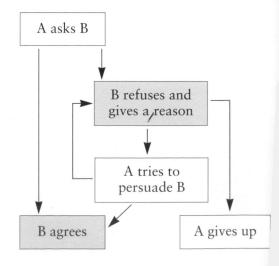

Talking points

Choose one of these topics. Take it in turns to say a sentence or two about it.

Rice: from the field to the table

Labour-saving devices

Last week's news

Bargains

Things that are a waste of money

The cost of living

Strict parents

What people do on holiday

Festivals

Words

1 What jobs do you do around the house?
   What jobs do other people do?
   Make two lists.

2 How many ways of paying for things can you think of?

3 Think of some things to take
   – to the beach
   – on a visit to London.

4 Answer these questions.
   What does an *untidy* person do?
   What happens in an *earthquake*?
   When do you get a *receipt*?
   What might you do if you go *sightseeing*?

2 On the phone

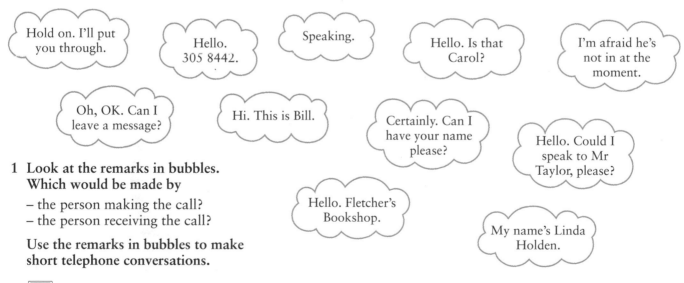

1 Look at the remarks in bubbles. Which would be made by

   – the person making the call?
   – the person receiving the call?

   Use the remarks in bubbles to make short telephone conversations.

   Now listen to the recording. Were the conversations similar to yours?

2 Work in pairs. Read your instructions and have two short telephone conversations.

Student A	Student B
Student A	*Student B*
1 Phone Harvey's Department Store and ask to speak to Mrs Davies.	1 You work at Harvey's Department Store. Mrs Davies is out having lunch. Ask if the caller wants to leave a message.
2 You're Sophie's mother/father. She's busy doing her homework. She can't come out tonight because she's got too much to do.	2 Phone your friend Sophie and ask her if she wants to go and see a film tonight.

7

Past and present

1 Ancient civilisations

used to • Past simple tense

1 *a* Look at the picture and read the three descriptions.
   Only one of them is true. Which one?

   b When do we use *used to*?

Detail from a scroll by the T'ang painter Chang Hsüan, 9th century AD

In ancient China, it was common for girls to get engaged at the age of 9 or 10. At the engagement ceremony, the women of the family used to hold up a length of cloth which the girl had to pass under. A bowl of flower petals, symbolising fertility, was placed on the cloth and the mother used to take petals from the bowl and scatter them over the girl's head.

In ancient China, ironing silk was a skilled job that was done by several people working together. The silk was so long that instead of using an ironing board, the women of the house used to iron it in mid-air. Two women pulled on the ends of the silk to stretch it out, while a third ironed it using a small pan filled with hot coals.

In ancient China, dining tables in wealthy households used to have handles, rather than legs. At mealtimes, the table was brought from the kitchen and two servants used to hold it for the entire length of the meal, while another served the different courses one at a time. Educated people used to eat standing up, as this was believed to help digestion.

2 Choose one of the pictures on page 116,
   and imagine what the people used to do.
   Write a few sentences to accompany the picture.

2 Changes

Present perfect tense

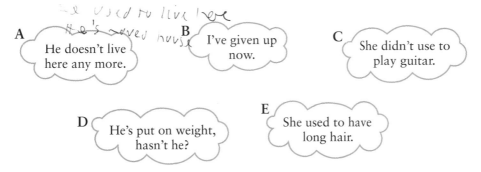

She used to ride a motorbike.

She's sold her motorbike now.

She doesn't ride a motorbike any longer.

1 *a* What is the difference between the three remarks above?

  b Look at the remarks below, and make two more sentences about each situation.

He used to live here
He's saved house

A He doesn't live here any more.

B I've given up now.

C She didn't use to play guitar.

D He's put on weight, hasn't he?

E She used to have long hair.

2 Work in pairs. You will see a picture of a couple sitting in their living room.

Student A: Look only at the picture on page 113, which shows how things used to be.

Student B: Look only at the picture on page 115, which shows how things are now.

How many changes can you find?

3 Preparations

Present perfect active & passive

Everything's ready for the wedding …

They're ready to set off on their journey …

The hotel's ready for the new holiday season …

The food has been delivered.

They've hired a new chef.

The pool has been filled.

The rooms have been redecorated.

They've ordered the flowers.

They've made some sandwiches.

The car's been serviced.

They've hired a photographer.

They've packed their cases.

1 Look at the sentences in the boxes. Which preparations do you think go with each? Add a few ideas of your own.

2 The teacher will give you a situation. Write a list of preparations you have made.

To make from scratch → cocinar desde la propretos naturales
a hazard → danger

4 For and against

1  You will hear people talking about these inventions, and saying whether they think they have had a good or bad effect on people's lifestyles.

  a Which invention is each speaker talking about?
     Does he/she think the effect has been good or bad?

  b Think of an argument that gives a *different* point of view about each invention.

2 Work in groups. Decide together where to mark each invention in the table.

	very good	*good*	*–*	*bad*	*very bad*
television					
calculators					
computers					
convenience food					
video recorders					

Grammar Checklist

used to

used to + *infinitive – for regular past events and past states.*

My grandfather **used to** walk to school.
    (*not* ... ~~was used to~~ ...)
I **used to** live in France (when I was a child).
I **didn't use to** smoke (but I do now).
Where **did** you **use to** spend your holidays?

Present perfect tense

have/has + *past participle – for talking about changes and recent events. (See also Unit 15.)*

He's (= he has) **given** up smoking.
They **haven't** painted the room yet.
Have you packed the suitcases?

Irregular verbs: see list on page 143.

not ... any more/longer

They **don't** live here **any longer**.
    (= They've moved away.)

He **doesn't** have a beard **any more**.
    (= He's shaved it off.)

Present perfect passive

have/has + **been** + *past participle*

They've painted the room.
→ The room **has been** painted.

Someone has ordered the books.
→ The books **have been** ordered.

See also Reference section, page 133.

Focus on Form

1 Forms of used to

Student A: Ask B about when he/she was seven years old.

Student B: Answer A's questions.

Examples:

A What TV programmes *did you use to* watch?

B | I *used to* watch a lot of cartoons.
     | I *didn't use to* watch much TV.

or

A *Did you use to* watch much TV?

B | No, not really.
     | Yes. I *used to* watch it every day after school.

a watching TV   *e* eating sweets
b going to bed   *f* holidays
c playing with toys *g* school
d reading   *h* homework

2 Present perfect tense

The picture shows A's flat as it was this morning.

Student A: It's B's job to clean your flat. Write a list of all the jobs you wanted him/her to do in your flat. Then find out how many of them he/she's done.

Student B: You've just finished cleaning A's flat. Write a list of the jobs you've done. Then answer A's questions.

Example:

A Have you changed the sheets?

B Yes I have.
     No I'm afraid I haven't.
     No I haven't, but I've made the bed.

Now compare your flat with someone else's. Which is cleaner?

3 Present perfect passive

Student A: Read out the sentences in Box A.

Student B: Complete each sentence using an item from Box B in the Present perfect passive.

Example:

A That building used to be a theatre …
B … but now it's been turned into a cinema.

A	B
That building used to be a theatre … There used to be a castle on that hill … He used to have a good job … This room used to have red wallpaper … There used to be a big tree in the square … We used to go for walks in that field … They used to let you smoke in the cinema … He didn't use to earn much money …	redecorate it pull it down cut it down promote him sack him turn it into a cinema ban it fence it off

4 Pronunciation

How do you say the words and phrases below?

a I <u>used to</u> drink coffee.

b I've She's He's They've
   He's packed the suitcase.
   John <u>has</u> left home.
   My parents <u>have</u> come to stay.

c The room's <u>been</u> cleaned.
   Ten people <u>have been</u> arrested.

▭ **Now listen and check your answers.**

1 Yellow Pages

NELSON PHOTOGRAPHY

Personal Attention –
Professional Results

Weddings
Portraits
Passports
Commercial
By
George L. Nelson

155 North High Street
Musselburgh, Midlothian
EH21 6AN

031-665 5058

FAX 031-665 5058
CELLNET (0860) 710319

Headline

FOR HAIR REFLECTING STYLE
63 SHANDWICK PLACE, EDINBURGH
TEL: 031–229 1582
CAMERON TOLL TEL: 664 6849

BONNYRIGG

Scott Christie B.D.S.
Dental Surgeon

64 HIGH STREET
BONNYRIGG

031-663 9271

*FAMILY DENTAL CARE
ALL EMERGENCIES SEEN*

THE ELECTRICAL REPAIR MAN EST 1974

**OFFICES
SHOPS
HOUSES**

Electrical
Repairs
& Installations.

031-229 8370

Estimates Free on New Work & Rewiring
A.A.E.S.   Mobile: 0850 423451
244 Morrison St. Edinburgh EH3 8DT

MUNRO CLEANERS

Bathgate	42 George Street	0506 630825
Broxburn	Unit 4, Argyll Court	0506 858630
Bruntsfield	141 Bruntsfield Pl	031-228 6365
City Centre	123 Hanover Street	031-226 2931
	3 Elm Row	031-556 0603
	90 Nicolson Street	031-667 4420
Corstorphine	12 Ormiston Terrace	031-334 6439
Cupar	8 Bonnygate	0334 55944
Dalkeith	9 High Street	031-654 1277
Davidson Mains	68 Main Street	031-336 2657
Dunfermline	14 East Port	0383 620457
Easter Road	7 Easter Road	031-661 5899
Glenrothes	6 Unicorn Way	0592 611468
Gorgie	156 Gorgie Road	031-313 2190
Haddington	31 Market Street	062082 4893
Haymarket	18/20 Dalry Road	031-337 0542
Kirkcaldy	77 High Street	0592 262227
	254a High Street	0592 269182
Leith	75 Gt. Junction St	031-554 3733
Linlithgow	73 High Street	0506 670660
Livingston	10 Almondvale South	0506 441351
Morningside	350 Morningside Rd	031-447 2140
Newington	95 Newington Rd	031-668 4767
Penicuik	24a John Street	0968 679834
Portobello	100 High Street	031-657 4958
St. Andrews	27 Church Street	0334 78831
Stockbridge	45 Deanhaugh St	031-332 3298
Tollcross	21 Home Street	031-229 0927

Contract Drycleaning Collection & Delivery Service
Curtain Cleaning, Pleating & Flame Proofing
Duvet & Pillow Renovation
17 Swanfield, Bonnington Rd, Leith. 031-554 3825

YELLOW PAGES®

EDINBURGH

It pays to

SPECIALEYES

Qualified Opticians · Free Frames
One Hour Service · Contact Lenses
Designer Frames

EDINBURGH 031-558 3306
31 St James Centre,
Edinburgh.

G. W. MARTIN LTD OF MORNINGSIDE

AA SPECIALIST

- SERVICING & REPAIRS OF MOST MAKES OF CARS
- FULL COMPREHENSIVE FACILITIES AVAILABLE
- STEERING, BRAKES, SUSPENSION, CLUTCHES ETC

031-447 6185

FAX: 031-452 8740 11 JORDAN LANE (OFF MORNINGSIDE ROAD) EDINBURGH

**M.O.T TESTING
WHILE-U-WAIT** (INCLUDING DIESEL TESTING)

---

1 Look at these advertisements from Yellow Pages. What services
do they offer? What can you have done at each place?

Example: At the photographer's you can have your photo taken.

2 Choose one of the advertisers and think of a reason for ringing
them up. What questions would you ask? What would you
expect them to ask you?

Now have a telephone conversation with your partner.

---

2 What's the system?

1 You will hear people explaining how to do these things in Britain.

   – use a public phone
   – use a public library
   – send a parcel abroad

   How do you think they will use the words in the box?

receiver	take out	join
registered	dial	customs form
stamps	weigh	reference section
pay a fine		

   Now listen to the recording.

2 Think of one of these services in your own country. How would you explain to a foreigner how to use it? Design a leaflet.

How to send a parcel abroad

● **Write the address clearly in block capitals.**

3 Public services

Yet again the crime rate is up:
Burglaries are UP by 4%.
Violent crime is UP by 6%.
And car crime is UP by a staggering 14%.

Most people in Britain still think our police are doing a good job, a survey reveals today.

Police are still prejudiced against members of ethnic minorities, and do not understand their special needs, a spokesman for the Asian

Most junior hospital doctors work 70 hours a week and some work as many as 90.

63-year-old Janet Gould has been waiting for more than TWO YEARS for a simple operation – and she's typical of thousands of others around

When asked about the rise in prescription charges, Mr Baker replied that children, old age pensioners, pregnant women and unemployed people do not pay for medicines at all.

1 Look at these newspaper reports about Britain. Which of them could be true of your country?

2 Think about the police, health and education services in your country. Give a mark out of 10 for each.

   Compare your marks with your partner's.

Why is it that after 5 years at school, some 10% of British children cannot read or write?

Many primary school classes still contain more than 30 pupils, in spite of a Government promise to

More secondary school students are going on to university and other forms of further education than ever before.

	Mark out of 10	Notes
Police		
Health		
Education		

---

4 Jobs we love to hate

It's a lonely life. Clive Brown at work.

HELP
NOBODY LOVES US!

They've got the jobs we love to hate ... from traffic warden to nightclub bouncer, we found out what it's like when nobody, but nobody, loves you.

READING

1 Read the opening descriptions of the three people's jobs. What do you think these expressions mean?

private eye   taking her life in her hands   a strapping 6ft 9in
insurance claims   like gold dust
tempers can flare

2 All three people answer the same six questions. What do you think the questions were?

3 Which of the people do you think

  a has the most dangerous job?   *c* is most interested in the money?
  b spends most time talking to people?   *d* is most interested in job security?

4 Which of these adjectives do you think describes each person best?

calm	friendly	cynical
cheerful	helpful	self-confident

LISTENING

1 ⌗ You will hear four people talking about jobs they 'love to hate'. What are the four jobs?

2 Which jobs do these statements apply to?

  a They try to sell you things you don't want.   *e* They keep you waiting.
  b They don't tell you what's going on.   *f* They ask stupid questions.
  c They disturb you when you're busy.   *g* You can't trust them.
  d They don't keep their promises.   *h* They waste your time and money.

JOB: PRIVATE INVESTIGATOR	JOB: TRAFFIC WARDEN	JOB: NIGHTCLUB BOUNCER
Name: Clive Brown, 44 **Qualifications:** police training plus common sense **Home life:** married with two children **Salary:** over £35,000 a year **Being a private eye in real life isn't nearly as exciting as it is in detective stories. Clive Brown is on call day and night, investigating large insurance claims, dishonest employees, and unfaithful husbands and wives.**	**Name:** Linda Jackson, 35 **Qualifications:** on-the-job training **Home life:** single **Salary:** £16,000 a year **For the past 13 years, traffic warden Linda Jackson has been taking her life in her hands. In the few square miles of city streets where 5ft 4in Linda has her beat, parking spaces are like gold dust and tempers can flare.**	(official title 'Persuader') **Name:** Jim Allen, 42 **Qualifications:** none, but all the right physical attributes **Home life:** married, no kids **Salary:** £65 a night **Bouncer Jim, a strapping 6ft 9in, has been standing on the door of the Black Cat nightclub in Leeds for the last 20 years making sure that trouble stays out and only the right kind of people get in.**
I became a private eye because I was unemployed and had a family to support. I used to be a policeman so this was an obvious business.	Basically for security. The company I worked for was making redundancies. Traffic wardens' money was good and so were the promotion prospects.	I wanted work where I could meet people as I do enjoy it very much. Obviously, I'm also pretty strong physically, being an ex-professional boxer and wrestler.
I might not admit I'm a private investigator, but there are plenty of ways to 'disguise' what I do, such as calling myself a 'security consultant'.	If I'm meeting someone for the first time I might say I work for the Civil Service. Then if they ask further I tell them because I'm quite proud of my job.	Well, I don't like to be too obvious at the club, but I'd never lie about my job. I'm not out to give people any trouble.
Oh, you bet! You come across a lot of rather unpleasant characters. Someone who's been battering his wife, for example, isn't going to think twice before he starts battering me!	I was very nearly attacked once, when I had to call the police to help me deal with a man who got extremely nasty. He was arrested – and he got a ticket from me as well!	Some people get a bit upset at the door and won't be told to go quietly. But I never use violence myself. If anyone starts a fight, I always call the police.
Not that I can think of, but, in fact, if I'm doing my job properly I shouldn't have much contact with the people I'm investigating. They shouldn't even be aware I'm interested in them!	Quite often I come up against people with a problem – someone ill at home, for example, and they have to get to the chemist. But I'd never stand there and argue or reduce them to tears. I just help as best I can.	No! To be a bouncer, you need to understand people and to know about life. I think I'm very tactful. If I made the customers cry I might as well be working on a building site.
Just every now and then, when a client's cheque bounces. That really brings the tears to my eyes! But, seriously, I try not to get emotionally involved in my job; otherwise I wouldn't be able to do it.	Some of the horrible things people say have upset me, but I wouldn't give them the satisfaction of crying. Anyway I'd look pretty stupid in a uniform sobbing on the street.	Do what?
I'd like to say the satisfaction of helping my fellow men and women, but to be honest the thing I really like best about it is the money it brings me.	Meeting people – I'm a real chatterbox and love talking. I used to be shy, but the job soon changed that!	The people, without a doubt! I can mix with the crowd for most of the time so it's a nice social job.

Imagining

1 What would you do?

would

Situation 1

Your 14-year-old daughter thinks that the only reason you have a phone is so that she can talk to her friends all evening. You've told her that she can't phone them any more – so now her friends phone her instead.

4.00pm What would you do?
This week the panel looks at some of the problems that parents have with children – and children have with parents.

1 Look at the first situation. You will hear part of a radio programme in which three people discuss what they would do. Who do you agree with most?

2 Choose one of the other situations. Say what you would and wouldn't do.

Situation 2

Some older pupils at school are bullying you. You would like to ask your parents' advice, but you're afraid that they might rush round to the school and make a big fuss, and that this might only make things worse.

Situation 3

Your 3-year-old daughter won't eat her meals. Apart from cheese, she will only eat 'junk food' like chips, crisps, cake, sweets and ice-cream. You've told her that she can't leave the table until she eats her meal, but that doesn't work: she just sits and looks at it without eating.

Situation 4

You belong to a very close family who have always done things together. You're 15 now, and you would like to spend more time with your friends, especially at weekends. But your parents always organise family activities that fill up the whole weekend, and say you're too young to go off on your own.

2 If …

2nd conditional

If human beings lived for 150 years…

If cigarettes were banned…

If people could communicate by telepathy…

If I saw a tarantula…

If I had six months to live…

If I met the President of the United States face to face…

1 Here are the beginnings of six *If* … sentences.
Why are the verbs in the Past tense?
How do you think the sentences might continue?

2 On a piece of paper, write the first part of an *If* … sentence, and give it to another student to complete.

3 Cool thinking

A NEW ICE AGE?

MOST OF THE TALK these days is about global warming. But in fact the opposite could happen: it would only take the tiniest change in the Earth's orbit round the Sun to bring another Ice Age. A change of as little as 5°C would have a dramatic effect on life on Earth.

1 Here's the first paragraph of a magazine article.

What do you think would happen if the temperature of the world fell by 5°C? Think about
– climate
– food
– people.
Now read the complete article on page 117.

2 How would a new Ice Age affect the place where you live?
How would it affect your own life?

4 Wishes

I wish I had a
better car.

I wish I didn't live in
such a cold climate.

I wish I could play
the guitar.

I wish I lived in a
smaller house.

I wish my children
would leave home.

I wish I had time to
do more exercise.

I wish I could take more
time off work.

1 Look at these wishes. Which ones do you think
   would be made by

   a a 20-year-old student?
   b her father, a 50-year-old businessman?

   [cassette icon] Now listen to the recording.
   What can you tell about the daughter and the father?

2 What do you wish?
   Write three sentences using *I wish* … and show them
   to your partner.

Grammar Checklist

would

What **would** you do?
I'**d** speak to his teacher.
I **wouldn't** let her use the phone.
   (*not* ~~wouldn't to let~~)

2nd conditional

If + *past*, … **would**(**n't**) … – *for imagining*
unreal or unlikely situations.

If I **won** the national lottery, I'**d** retire.
   (*not* ~~If I would win~~ …)
If I **had** a car, I'**d** take you to the station.
If you **didn't drink** so much coffee, you'**d**
   sleep better.
The roads **wouldn't** be so crowded if they
   built a by-pass.

I wish

I **wish** + *past* – *for talking about the present.*
I wish I **had** more friends.
I wish the roads **weren't** so crowded.

I **wish** + **could/would** – *for things you want to
do and things you want to happen.*
I wish I **could** go abroad.
I wish they'**d** build a by-pass.

See also Reference section, page 134.

Focus on Form

1 Questions with would

Find out whether your partner would do these things.

a give a lift to a hitch-hiker at night
b give money to a beggar in the street
c swim in the sea in winter
d cheat in an examination
e drive a car after drinking alcohol
f give up a seat on a bus for an elderly person
g kill someone in self-defence

Which of them would you do yourself?

2 1st & 2nd conditional

Look at these two conditional sentences. What is the difference?

1 If they *offer* me the job, I'*ll* probably take it.
2 Of course, if someone *offered* me a better job, I'*d* probably take it.

Now complete these *If ...* sentences.

a ... I'll give you a lift to the station.
b ... I'd hand it in to the police.
c If you carry on working like this ...
d ... no-one would need to learn English.
e If they weren't so rude to everyone ...
f If you don't apologise ...
g ... I'll come round and see you.
h ... you'd feel much better.

3 Advice: 2nd conditional

In pairs, make *If ...* sentences giving advice.

Student A: Choose items from the *Advice* box. Begin the sentence using *If* + past.

Student B: Complete the sentence with a suitable item from the *Reason* box.

Example:

A If you turned the sofa on its side ...
B ... it would go through the door.

Advice
Turn the sofa on its side.
Take your jacket off.
Don't hit your children.
Take your dog for a walk.
Get a diary.
Don't drink so much coffee.
Leave a key with a neighbour.
Don't leave food lying around.
Don't play music after midnight.

4 Wishes

Make sentences with *I wish ...* for each situation.

Example: *It's cloudy; the water's cold; you can't go swimming.*

I wish it wasn't so cloudy.
I wish the sun would come out.
I wish the water was warmer.
I wish we could go swimming.

a You're shy; you want to meet more people; no-one invites you out.
b You live with your parents; you want to leave home; you haven't got much money.
c Everything costs too much; you pay a lot of tax; you can't afford a holiday.
d You're on a desert island; it's very hot; you haven't got any books with you; you want to escape.

5 Pronunciation

How do you say the words and phrases below?

a Would you help them?
It would look better if you washed it.
What would you do?
Where would you go?

b I wouldn't go home.
It wouldn't help.

c I wish I could sing.
I wish we could visit them.

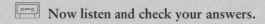 Now listen and check your answers.

Reason
Your parents would be able to get in.
It would go through the door.
You wouldn't forget so many appointments.
You wouldn't have mice in your flat.
They wouldn't be frightened of you.
You'd be more popular with your neighbours.
You'd sleep better.
You'd feel more comfortable.
It wouldn't bark so much.

1 I don't know what it's called but ...

1 *a* ⌨ You will hear students describing five objects they don't know the names of in English.
Which objects do they describe?

b Describe the other things in the pictures.

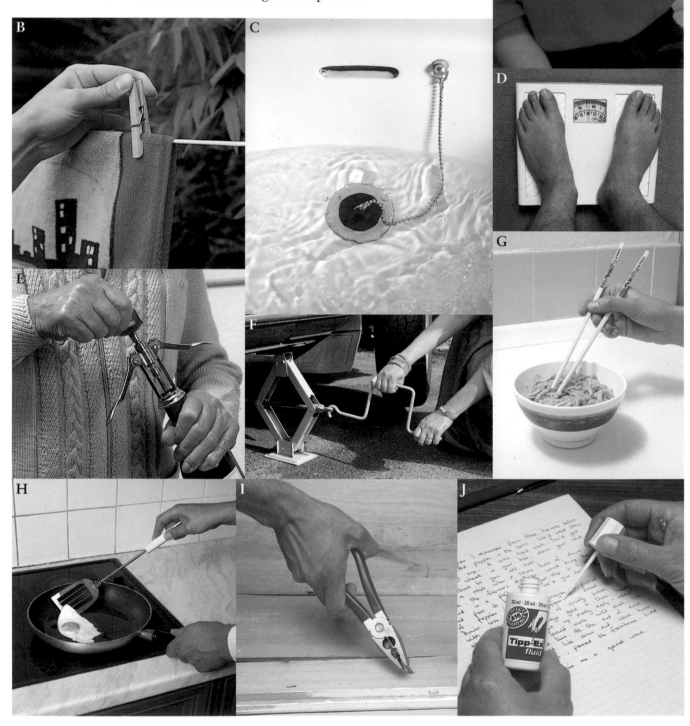

2 Think of three common objects whose names you don't know in English, and write a sentence describing each one.

Find out if other students know what your objects are called.

2 Things with a purpose

1 Use one word from each box to make objects that you might find
   - in an office
   - in a handbag
   - in a kitchen.

2 Can you think of two other kinds of
   - paper?
   - knife?
   - book?

A
filing   typing   word
food   hair
address   frying
phone   car   tin
reading   carving

B
keys   opener
pan   paper   glasses
knife   brush
processor
cabinet   book

3 Things for sale

1 Look at these advertisements. What questions might you ask the owners?

SPANISH GUITAR

Good condition. With case.

£50

Phone Steve at 325444

PUPPIES
FOR SALE

**Contact: Jean Wright
Phone: 987304**

FOR SALE

1976 VOLKSWAGEN

Dark green. Low mileage.

£120 o.n.o.

Phone: 331865 (after 5 pm)

SECOND-HAND

TYPEWRITER

Good working condition.
Recently cleaned and repaired.
Ideal for typing practice.

£25   Tel : 331256

BRASS BED
FOR SALE

150 years old. Genuine antique.
With mattress.

£150

phone: 322113

2 In pairs, choose one of the advertisements.

Student A: You're interested in buying the item. Find out more about it.

Student B: You want to sell the item. Answer A's questions.

4 Great ideas?

READING

Here are three ideas from inventors who lived in Victorian times. Do you think they would work? What problems do you think there might be?

A SPHERICAL, TRANSPARENT VELOCIPEDE

Imagine a hollow sphere made of some transparent but strong material, with a built-in door, and a seat attached to the sides, as shown.

Once inside, the rider simply 'walks' down the side of the sphere and the sphere starts to move forwards. If he wants to go right or left, he just leans his body slightly in the desired direction and the sphere will follow. To stop, he simply presses his feet against the place where the sphere touches the ground. If he wants to go backwards, he simply reverses his steps and the sphere will respond immediately.

But that is not all. He arrives at a river—let us suppose that it is not too wide—and the rider, going as fast as he can, rolls down the bank with enough speed to bring him to the other side of the river. The sphere floats on the water and continues to revolve until it has reached the opposite bank.

For this to work, the sphere must, of course, be airtight. But this is not a serious problem, as it contains more than 140 cubic feet of air—enough for the rider to keep breathing for up to two hours. [1884]

LISTENING

You will hear three people commenting on the three inventions.

1 What problems do they identify for each one?
   Write three lists.

2 Did you think of any problems that the speakers didn't?

A LIFE-PRESERVER

Mr Traugott Beek of Newark, New Jersey, has invented a floating life-preserver, which gives complete protection to people who have been shipwrecked. The upper section is large enough for the wearer to be able to move his head and arms about, and a month's supply of food and drinking-water can also be stored in it. The cover can be closed in rough weather, and the wearer can see through the window in the front, and breathe through a curved pipe. The life-preserver is made of waterproof cloth attached to circular metal tubes, which protect the wearer against sharp rocks and hungry fish. [1877]

Adapted from *Victorian Inventions* by Leonard de Vries, 1991.

A NATURAL FLYING MACHINE

Baltimore, 30th August, 1865

Dear Editor—

I would like to suggest an idea for a natural flying machine.

There are many birds, such as the brown eagle, which are both strong and can fly long distances. If these birds can carry up to 20 pounds each (we know that they are strong enough to carry off babies and lambs) one would need ten such eagles to carry an adult person through the air.

The eagles would have jackets fitted round their bodies, attached to circular metal tubes. These tubes would carry a metal basket large enough to hold a man. Strings passing through the hollow tubes would allow the passenger to control the direction of flight by pulling the head of the bird to one side or the other.

Would not this invention lead to an extremely simple and inexpensive means of air transport?

1 Were they right?

will do • will be done

The 1990s: Decade of Depression

▼ The depressed '90s
The 1990s will be a period of depression, affecting the whole world. Many large corporations will be wiped out and millions of jobs will be lost. Prices will fall and taxes will rise sharply.

▼ City violence
Large cities will become so violent that they will be very unpleasant places to live in. As a result, people who can afford it will move out of the city altogether and settle in smaller towns.

▼ Legalised drugs
During the depression of the 1930s, the ban on alcohol was lifted in the USA. In the same way, the ban on illegal drugs will be lifted during the depression of the 1990s, in an attempt to control violent crime and raise money.

▼ The changing world map
The 1990s will be a profitable time for map-makers. We will see the break-up not just of the Soviet Union, but of India, Canada, China, Yugoslavia, Ethiopia and other countries.

▼ Nuclear terrorism
Governments will find it more and more difficult to fight terrorism. Terrorist groups will become more powerful and more dangerous. They will manage to obtain nuclear and chemical weapons, and won't be afraid to use them.

▼ The rise of religion
During the 1990s, people in many countries will turn more and more to religion. Religion – particularly Islam, but other religions as well – will become increasingly important in world politics.

Adapted from *The Great Reckoning* by James Dale Davidson & William Rees-Mogg, 1991.

1 The predictions in the text come from a book which was written in 1990.

Which of the predictions do you think

– have already come true?
– might still come true?
– probably won't come true?

2 What is the difference between the verbs in these two sentences?

Prices *will fall*. Millions of jobs *will be lost*.

Find two other examples of each structure in the text.

Now make some predictions of your own.

2 Hopes and expectations

expect & hope

1 You've been invited to a party by some people you don't know very well. Which of these thoughts do you think would go through your mind?

I expect I'll meet lots of interesting people.

I don't expect I'll enjoy it much.

I hope there's someone there that I know.

I hope the food's good.

I hope I don't have to dance.

I hope there won't be too many people there.

2 What would you hope or expect in these situations? Write down your thoughts.
- You're about to go for a job interview.
- It's your birthday next week.
- A friend's children are coming to stay for the weekend.
- You're you, now.

3 In five years' time

will be doing • will have done

1 [cassette] You will hear someone being interviewed about her present life and future plans. What does she say about
- work?   – travel?
- marriage?   – a place to live?
- children?   – money?

Think of her in five years' time. What will her life be like? What will she be doing? What will she have done?

2 Now think of yourself in five years' time. Which of these things do you think will be true?

	I'll be married.
	I'll still be living in the same place.
	I will have travelled round the world.
	I'll have three children.
	I'll be working in an office.
	I will have written a novel.

What else will you be doing?
What else will you have done?

Compare your answers with your partner's.

4 Survival

1 There are four ways of completing the piece of advice in the table. What are they?

You should wear a life jacket …	
… because	you might drown.
… Otherwise	you don't drown.
… in case	the boat might capsize.
… so that	the boat capsizes.

Now give reasons for these pieces of advice.

a You should have a radio with you …
b You should make sure the boat's got an engine …
c You should carry a compass …
d You should take some warm clothes with you …

2 What advice might you give to one of these people?

– someone who wants to cross the Sahara Desert
– someone planning to go across Europe on a motorbike
– someone who wants to spend the summer in Britain

Grammar Checklist

will, might & won't

+ active infinitive

They'll probably **give** him the job.
There **will be** more cars on the road.
You **might feel** thirsty.
I **won't see** them till next year.

+ passive infinitive

The book **will be** published next year.
You **might be** attacked.
Bus fares **won't be** increased.

expect & hope

I expect
I **don't** expect | he'll come to the party.

I hope | he comes / he **doesn't** come | to the party.
(not I don't hope …)

Future continuous tense

will + be + -ing – *for things that **will be going on** at a point in the future.*

They'll still **be living** here next summer.
I'll **be waiting** at the station at 4 o'clock.

Future perfect tense

will + have + past participle – *for things that **will be completed** at a point in the future.*

He'll **have left** school by then.
I **won't have** finished it by lunchtime.

Linking expressions

You should wear a coat **because** it **might** rain.
You should wear a coat **in case** it **rains**.
(not … it will rain.)

Take a map. **Otherwise** you **might** get lost.
Take a map **so that** you **don't** get lost.

See also Reference section, page 135.

Focus on Form

1 Will do & will be done

Complete these sentences, using verbs from the box (1) in the active (2) in the passive.

cancel	sell	send to prison
sack	steal	take to hospital

Example: *When they realise we're missing …*

… they'll rescue us.
… we'll be rescued.

a If they catch him …
b If she turns up late again …
c When the puppies are six weeks old …
d If they don't sell more tickets …
e As soon as the ambulance arrives …
f If you leave your car unlocked overnight …

2 I expect & I hope

Student A: Do you expect these things will happen during your lifetime? Write sentences with *I expect*.

Student B: Do you hope these things will happen during your lifetime? Write sentences with *I hope*.

> There'll be a world war.

> They'll find a cure for cancer.

> Smoking will be made illegal.

> Elephants will become extinct.

> We'll make contact with beings from another planet.

Now compare your hopes and expectations.

3 Will/might be doing

Picture yourself at the times below. What do you think you'll be doing? Compare your answers with your partner's.

Example: *five minutes after this lesson ends*

I'll probably be waiting for the bus.
I might be having a cup of coffee.
I'll still be sitting here.

a five minutes after this lesson ends
b at 10.00 tonight
c tomorrow morning at 7.45
d next Saturday at 11.00 a.m.
e next Sunday at 3.30 p.m.
f at this time next week
g at midnight on December 31st

4 Will have done

Think of three things that these people *will* (*probably*) *have done* in five years' time.

Example:
Julia will have stopped wearing nappies.

Julia, 1, baby   Ian, 14, schoolboy

Mary, 19, student   Tom, 21, unemployed

5 In case & so that

Give advice based on these situations, using *in case* or *so that*.

Example: *They might keep you waiting.*

You should take a book …
    … in case they keep you waiting.
    … so that you don't get bored.

a They might not have a key.
b The traffic might be heavy.
c It might be muddy.
d They might not provide a meal.
e The weather might change.
f They might not know the way.

6 Pronunciation

How do you say the words and phrases below?

a I expect he'll write to you.
    I don't expect they'll win.

b I'll   he'll   she'll   they'll
    I'll be waiting.
    Mary will be working.

c I will have finished by then.

d You should take some water with you …
    … in case you feel thirsty.
    … so that you don't get thirsty.

 Now listen and check your answers.

12 Accidents

1 Narrow escapes

1 You will hear three people talking about narrow escapes they have had.

   a Look at the pictures. What do you think happened?
Use words from the box to help you.

ambulance	drown	smoke
catch fire	choke	slip
fire brigade	swallow	

   b ▭ Now listen to the stories.

2. Think of a narrow escape that you (or someone you know) has had,
and make some notes about it.

   Tell other students what happened.

2 Emergency

How good would you be in an emergency? Write down what you would do
(and what you wouldn't do) in these situations.

1 You're out walking and you get bitten in the leg by a poisonous snake.

3 You're in a hotel room on the 5th floor and the fire alarm goes. You see smoke coming under your door.

4 Someone in your family knocks a pan of boiling water off the cooker. The water goes over his/her arm.

2 You're preparing food in the kitchen when you accidentally cut yourself deeply on the hand.

5 You find an elderly relative lying on the floor. She tells you that she thinks she's had a heart attack.

Now change papers with someone else, and check their answers at the back of the book.
Give up to five points for each.

3 Bad driving

1 Fill the gaps using verbs from the box.

turn	overtake	run over
crash	miss	accelerate
skid	brake	swerve

2 *a* Look at these accidents. How do you think they happened?

b In pairs, choose one of the accidents. Imagine you are the two people involved. Try to decide whose fault it was.

He suddenly pulled out of a side road and I had to .... to avoid him.

He .... hard and managed to stop in time. But it was close – he only .... me by a few inches.

She just wouldn't let me get past. Every time I tried to .... her, she ....

She suddenly .... left without indicating, and almost .... two pedestrians.

He was going much too fast. He .... on the ice and .... straight into the back of me.

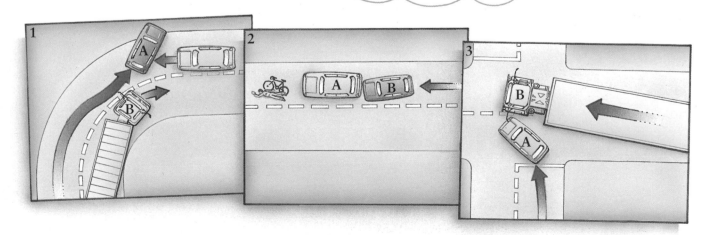

4 You're on your own

READING

1 Look at the headlines and the pictures. What is the story about?

2 Now read the opening paragraph.
   When Les Rhoades had a heart attack
   – what were he and Alan Anderson doing?
   – what did Anderson do?
   – what did Robert Legge do?

3 Now read the rest of the article.
   Which of these sentences are true of
   – Anderson?   – Legge?   – neither of them?

a He had never been in a plane before.	e He gave very clear instructions.
b He didn't know how to use the radio.	f He was terrified.
c He was a flying instructor.	g He made a perfect landing.
d He took off as soon as he heard the emergency call.	h He wants to learn how to fly.
	i He was shocked by his experience.

4 What was particularly impressive about the behaviour of
   – Anderson?   – Legge?

LISTENING

🎦 You will hear a reconstruction of part of the radio conversation between Legge and Anderson.

Before you listen, read the notes in the box.

Now listen to the recording. What does Legge tell Anderson to do at each of the stages 1–4 in the picture?

> **When you're flying a plane ...**
> - ... you hold the *control column*. Move it forward to drop the nose of the plane; pull it back to raise it.
> - ... you *bank* (or turn) by moving the control column left or right.
> - ... you open the *throttle* to speed up, and close it to slow down.
> - ... you control the *rudder* with *rudder pedals*; when you're on the ground, these act as brakes.

PASSENGER LANDS PLANE AFTER PILOT DIES

It's the air passenger's nightmare ... the pilot collapses and you are forced to seize the controls to save your own life. For Alan Anderson, 24, it became reality when his girlfriend's father Les Rhoades suffered a fatal heart attack at 2,200 ft over the Welsh coast on Sunday. The pilot of a second light aircraft, Robert Legge, responded to his radio call for help and, trailing behind, calmly gave instructions on how to land.

Alan Anderson: "I'll never fly again"

ALAN ANDERSON had never flown before. So he was looking forward to an exciting time when his future father-in-law, Les Rhoades, aged 63, invited him up for a ride in his light plane. What he hadn't expected was that Mr Rhoades would suffer a heart attack while they were in the air. Fortunately for Mr Anderson, Mr Rhoades had shown him how to operate the radio, so he was able to radio for help.

MAYDAY MAYDAY

Robert Legge, an instructor with the Cardiff Flying School who was in a plane a few miles away, was asked to help by air traffic controllers after they received an emergency call from Mr Anderson, saying: "Mayday, Mayday, my father-in-law has had a heart attack and I don't know how to fly."

Mr Legge pulled alongside Mr Anderson's plane and told him by radio how to fly the aircraft. He took

him through a practice landing and then helped him bring the plane down safely at Cardiff Airport just after 7 p.m.

INCREDIBLE FEAT

Mr Legge said last night: "It was an incredible feat for anyone, let alone someone for the first time ever in a light aircraft. He was fantastically calm. When I kept telling him what controls to use, the repeated reply was 'OK, but I've never done this before', but he never sounded frightened."

He added: "We had one chance to get it right and, thank God, we succeeded. The worst bit was coming

over the runway for the landing when I felt as though I was no longer in control, but he made a perfect landing. He did marvellously well."

DEEP SHOCK

After his ordeal, Mr Anderson was put under sedation for deep shock, and is now resting at his fiancée's home near Cardiff. He said yesterday: "After what I have been through, nothing will get me on a plane again. I've never been so terrified in my whole life, but I knew I had to keep calm." And he thanked Mr Legge, saying: "I didn't have a clue what to do, but Robert put me at ease and I just gritted my teeth and concentrated on the job in hand."

Robert Legge: he flew alongside

The plane's cockpit: a nightmare line-up of knobs, dials and lights

Find out

1 A What can you remember about your
   early childhood?
  B Help A to remember by asking
   questions.

2 Find out what other students would do
  – if they were stuck in a lift
  – if they won £1 million
  – if someone pulled out a knife in the
   street and said 'Hand over your money.'

3 A Imagine yourself at the age of 65.
   What will you be like? What will you be
   doing? What will you have done?
   Answer B's questions.
  B Ask as many different questions as you
   can.

Role-play

1 A You're having a party tonight. What
   have you done to prepare for it? Make
   some notes, then answer B's questions.
  B Write a list of things for A to do. Then
   check whether he/she's done them.

2 A You've got a bad toothache. Ring up the
   dentist and make an appointment.
  B You're the dentist. You're very busy. Do
   your best to give A an appointment.

3 A You're going camping for the first time.
   Ask B for advice about what to do,
   what to take, what to expect.
  B You're an experienced camper. Answer
   A's questions, and give reasons for your
   advice.

Conversational English

1 Making suggestions

1 🔲 You will hear some suggestions.
Which suggestions do you think go with each situation?

Make a list of the structures you heard.

2 Work in groups. How many suggestions can you make for each of
these situations? Use a range of structures for each one.
  – It's your teacher's birthday next week.
  – One of you is thinking of taking a holiday job.
  – You want to give a party with a difference.

Talking points

Choose one of these topics. Take it in turns to say a sentence or two about it.

The past five years: good and bad changes

Making an international phone call

A job you wouldn't like to have

'I wish ...'

Buying things second-hand

Next year's news

'I hope ...'

Dos and Don'ts on the road

Words

1 **Why might you go to these places?**
   - a dry cleaner's   – a hairdresser's
   - a photographer's   – an optician's

2 **Add words to these lists.**
   - library, borrow ...
   - wood, metal ...
   - fire, burn ...

3 **What are the following?**
   - a pencil sharpener   – a carving knife
   - a dishwasher   – a chessboard

4 **Say what might happen if**
   - you mend a light without switching it off
   - you go sailing without a life jacket
   - you give a small child peanuts to eat
   - you overtake someone on a bend.

2 Finding things in common

1 *a* Look at the three remarks on the left, and find two replies for each.

   What replies would *you* give?

> I love computer games.

> I've never been to Los Angeles.

> My dad was really strict when I was little.

> Mine wasn't. He let me do whatever I liked.

> I have. I went when I was a baby.

> I don't. I think they're a complete waste of time.

> So was mine. He was always telling me what to do.

> So do I. I spend hours playing them.

> Nor have I, but I'd love to go.

b Work in pairs. Have similar conversations starting with these remarks.
   - I've *seen / never seen* a UFO.
   - I *was/wasn't* a very quiet child.
   - My mother *goes out / doesn't go out* to work.
   - I'd *like / wouldn't like* to live in Hawaii.
   - I *believe / don't believe* in ghosts.
   - I'm / I'm not interested in politics.

2 Work in groups. Think of one or two sentences of your own – facts about yourself, opinions, things you like or don't like. Find out how much you have in common with the others.

Comparing and evaluating

1 National differences

Comparison structures

1 You will hear people from France, Japan and the USA talking about differences between Britain and their own country.
What do you think their opinions will be? Complete the sentences.

.... is much more crowded than Britain.

Britain's a safer place to live than ....

In Britain, people have much more respect for the law than in ....

In ...., people are more interested in each other than they are in Britain.

The British don't spend as much time over their meals as the ....

People aren't as honest in Britain as they are in ....

Now listen to the recording and see if you were right. Do they mention any other differences?

2 Write down three differences between your own country and another country.

2 Who does it best?

Adjectives & adverbs

Amanda

I'm a faster swimmer than Brian, but he's better at singing than I am. His English isn't as fluent as mine, and you should see his handwriting – I write much more neatly!

Brian

Poor Claire – she can hardly sing at all, and she doesn't swim very fast either – not as fast as I do, anyway! But she speaks English more fluently than I do.

Claire

I wish I could sing as beautifully as Amanda – unfortunately I've got a very bad singing voice. But I speak English better than she does, and I certainly write more neatly!

	swimming	singing	English	writing
Amanda				
Brian				
Claire				

1 Which of these three people

  – is the fastest swimmer?
  – is the best at singing?
  – speaks English the most fluently?
  – has the neatest handwriting?

2 Work in threes.
   Talk about the same activities. Find out who does each of them best.

3 Not good enough

too & enough

He spoke too fast.

There wasn't enough food.

The music was much too loud.

There wasn't enough for the children to do.

It was quite interesting, but it went on far too long.

It wasn't warm enough to sit on the beach.

Too many people were smoking.

The room wasn't big enough.

1 Look at the complaints in the bubbles. Which pictures do you think they go with?

What else do you think was wrong?

2 Continue these remarks with a complaint using *too* or *enough*.

  a My first English lesson was a disaster …
  b I'll never go to that restaurant again …
  c If you carry on like this, you're going to have a heart attack …
  d Working conditions at the factory are terrible …

4 Awards

Musician of the Year

Funniest TV Show

Best Night Spot

Best Place to Live

Best Restaurant

Politician of the Year

1 Who or what would you nominate for these awards?
   Think of one or two candidates for each.

2 Work in groups. Choose one of the awards, and together decide which
   candidate should win it.

   Tell the rest of the class which candidate you chose, and why.

Grammar Checklist

Comparative adjectives & adverbs

Adjectives: bigger, easier; **more** interesting, **more**
careful.
Adverbs: faster, louder; **more** easily, **more**
carefully.
Irregular: good → **better**; well → **better**.

Comparative structures

... -er than
more ... than

Your room is | tidier / more attractive | **than** mine.

She drives | faster / more slowly | **than** I do.

as ... as ...
He's **as** tall **as** his father.
I'm nearly **as** old **as** you.
My room **isn't as** tidy **as** yours.
I don't drive **as** fast **as** she does.

Big & small differences

Your room is **far/much** tidier than mine.
My room isn't **nearly** as tidy as yours.

She drives **slightly/a bit** faster than I do.
I don't drive **quite** as fast as she does.

too & not enough

too + *adjective or adverb*
too much/many + *noun*

You work **too** hard.
It's **too** cold to swim.
There are **too many** people here.

not + *adjective or adverb* + **enough**
not enough + *noun*

The table isn't big **enough**.
He couldn't walk fast **enough**.
There isn't **enough** food to eat.

See also Reference section, page 136.

Focus on Form

1 Big and small differences

...	slightly a bit	Adj. + -er	than ...
	much far	more + Adj.	

Student A: **Can you guess the answers to the questions below? Do you think there's a big difference or a small one? Use the structures in the table.**

Student B: **Look at the facts on page 118. Tell A if he/she is right or wrong.**

Example: *Which is bigger, the Atlantic or the Pacific?*

The Pacific is much bigger than the Atlantic.

a Which country uses more nuclear power, France or Spain?
b Who lived longer, Elvis Presley or Mozart?
c Which is more fattening, flour or sugar?
d Which is bigger, Los Angeles or San Francisco?
e Who drink more alcohol, the British or the French?
f Which is higher, Mount Fuji or Mount Kilimanjaro?

2 Not as ... as ...

Write sentences with *not as ... as ...* based on the facts in Exercise 1.
Example:
The Atlantic isn't (nearly) as big as the Pacific.

3 Adverbs

Look at these adjectives. Write the adverb forms in the table.

	Adverb	Comparative adverb
quick	quickly	
fast	fast	
slow		
hard		
early		
clear		
good		

Use three comparative adverb forms in sentences of your own.

4 Finding fault: too & enough

What might be wrong with the things below?
Complain about them using *too* and *not enough*.
Example: *a plate of hamburgers and chips*

The chips aren't hot enough.
The hamburgers are too greasy.
There aren't enough chips.
There's too much ketchup.

a a cup of coffee
b the local bus service
c a bar
d your car
e your neighbours

5 Too/enough to ...

Student A: **Start a sentence using *too* or *not enough*.**

Student B: **Complete the sentence using *to* + infinitive.**

Example:
A The wall isn't high enough ...
B ... to keep burglars out.

A	B
The wall isn't very high.	She doesn't go out on her own.
I don't play very well.	I can't go on holiday this year.
The water's cold.	It won't keep burglars out.
She speaks fast.	Children shouldn't play in it.
She's rather busy.	I can't understand her.
I haven't got much money.	Don't swim in it.
That road's dangerous.	She can't talk to you just now.
My mother's very old.	I won't get in the team.

6 Pronunciation

How do you say the words and phrases below?

a Japan's much safer than the USA.
  France is a bit bigger than Britain.

b She doesn't play as well as I do.

c It's not fast enough.
  There aren't enough people.

d The wall's too high to jump over.

Now listen and check your answers.

14 The media

1 In print

1 Look at the picture. What are the people reading?

2 Work in groups. Answer the questionnaire.
   How much have you got in common?

Questionnaire

1 Which of your national newspapers do you think is
   – the best?
   – the worst?

2 Which of these is true?
   a I buy a newspaper every day
   b I buy one sometimes.
   c I read someone else's.

3 Which part of the newspaper do you turn to first?
   Which parts do you *never* read?

4 Do you buy
   – a weekly magazine?
   – a monthly magazine?
   What do you like about them?

5 You're in a dentist's waiting room, and these are the only magazines on the table. Which of them would you read?

ON OTHER PAGES

Home news	2–5
International news	6–10
Financial news	11–12
Leading articles	13
Letters	14
Arts & Entertainment	15–16
Obituaries	17
Classified advertisements	17
Horoscope	18
Cartoons	18
TV and Radio	19–20
Sport	21–24
Weather	24
Crossword	24

Now imagine that your group is going on a long train journey. You can only afford *one* newspaper and *one* magazine. Can you agree on what to buy?

2 Changing channels

1 ⌷▭ You will hear someone changing TV channels. Match what you hear with the programmes in the box.

> cartoon
> chat show
> comedy show
> crime series
> documentary
> game show
> news broadcast
> soap
> sports programme

Now listen again, and imagine what the person can see on the screen.

2 Which of the programmes would you carry on watching? Does your partner agree with your choice?

3 On the line

Leave Us Alone, Say Royal Family

SOAP STAR'S SUICIDE: 'I BLAME THE PRESS' SAYS GIRLFRIEND

TEENAGER KILLS 5 AFTER WATCHING VIOLENT TV FILMS

LOVE SCENE CUT FROM TV PLAY

EXCLUSIVE!
SECRET TOXIC WASTE DUMPS: THEY *DO* EXIST
We reveal the truth behind the lies

SECRET SERVICE DOCUMENTARY BANNED
Not in the national interest, says Minister

1 Look at these newspaper headlines.
What do you think the stories are behind the headlines?

2 How free do you think the media should be? Mark your position on the line.
What do you think the media should/shouldn't be allowed to do?

The Press and TV should be allowed to do whatever they like.		There should be very strict controls on the Press and TV.

Find someone whose position on the line is different from yours. Compare your opinions.

4 Easy listening

What do trains, frogs, Abba, counting sheep, motorbikes and a mother's heartbeat all have in common?

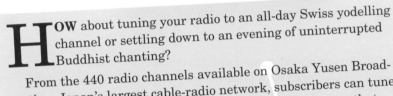

HOW about tuning your radio to an all-day Swiss yodelling channel or settling down to an evening of uninterrupted Buddhist chanting?

From the 440 radio channels available on Osaka Yusen Broadcasting, Japan's largest cable-radio network, subscribers can tune into a channel featuring 24 hours of croaking frogs, or one that consists of the sound of trains pulling in and out of stations.

As well as the sounds of cicadas or percolating coffee, Osaka Yusen offers nearly 100 channels of announcer-free jazz, rock, classical music, Second World War military marches, and folk music from all over the world. Sheena Easton, Abba and Lionel Richie each have entire channels to themselves, although the repetition rate must be almost as high as that of an in-flight music channel. One student says that he most often listens to the channel that plays the sound of a revving motorcycle engine.

For those in search of more intellectual background sounds for their dinner parties, there is always the abacus-lesson channel or a range of talks on spiritual development. But anyone tired of all the above should adjust their sets to 'drowsing channels' and tune into the sheep-counting station, for example, which features a mature male voice slowly counting from one to a thousand. Then he starts again. In the background, there is the faint sound of a train moving slowly along a railway track.

For busy executives wishing to calm down after an awful day at work, there is a channel of slow synthesiser music, and another carrying only the sound of a mother's heartbeat. According to the company: 'Babies listen to this noise before they are born. It's a natural relaxant.'

READING

1 What is the answer to the question above the text on page 66?

2 Which of these sentences about the text are true, and which are false?

  a You can only listen to the radio channels at certain times of the day.
  b On the music channels, the music is introduced by disc jockeys.
  c 'Drowsing channels' are intended to help you get to sleep.
  d The heartbeat channel is for babies only.
  e There are nearly 100 channels available altogether.

3 What are these sounds like?

  – *yodelling*
  – Buddhist *chanting*
  – *croaking* frogs
  – *percolating* coffee
  – a *revving* motorcycle engine

4 Look at the list on the right. Why do you think people would want to tune in to these channels?

  C2   C17   H29   J32

5 Choose three channels from the list that you think you would enjoy.

LISTENING

[cassette icon] You will hear two foreigners who live in Japan talking about cable radio channels they listen to. The recording is in four short parts.

1 What channels do they mention? What do they use them for? Complete the table.

	Channels	*What do they use them for?*
Part 1		
Part 2		
Part 3		
Part 4		

2 Which of these words were used in each part? How did each speaker use them?

alarm clock   background music   phone box
atmosphere   meeting   pop star

Now listen again and check your answers.

Tropical
C1 Sea, Waves, Seashore
C2 Sea, Waves, Seashore + Music
Japanese Sounds
C3 Waterwheel, Waterfall
C4 Waterwheel, Waterfall + Music
Seasonal Music
C5 New Year's Tunes
C6 Music for the The Dolls' Festival and The Boys' Festival
C7 Hawaiian, Christmas

Background Music
C17 Morning Music with Birdcalls
C18 Midnight Music
C19 Social Dance Music
C20 Sound of Steam Locomotives
Karaoke
C23 Duets
C24 Popular
C25 Lessons in Karaoke

Music for Places of Business
G28 Office (Slow)
G29 Office (Up-tempo)
G30 Bank (Slow)
G31 Bank (Moderate)
G32 Bank (Up-tempo)

For Children
H23 Japanese and Foreign Legends
H24 Songs from TV Cartoons
H26 Nursery Rhymes and Songs
H27 Music for Babies
H28 Bedtime Stories
H29 Lullabies
H30 Mother's Heartbeat

Spiritual Music
H31 Self-realization
H32 Cultivating Innate Ability
H33 Concentration (Enhancing Creativity)
H34 Spiritual Stability (Enhancing Patience)
H35 Easing Stress
Drowsing
H36 Drowsing
H37 Philosophical Talks
H38 Counting Sheep

Sounds of Nature
J21 Rural Scenery (Cows, Insects ...)
J22 Rain, Wind, Thunder
J23 Port Town (Ships, Sea ...)
J24 Summer Scenery (Cicadas, Frogs ...)
J25 Rooster Calls and Bells Ringing
Ceremonial Music
J26 Birthday Song
J27 Japanese Wedding
J29 Hymns

For Alibis
J30 Pachinko & Mah-jong
J31 Telephone Booth
J32 Bar, Coffee Shop
Fun Corner
J33 Jokes & Music
J34 Scary Music
J35 Movie Information
J37 Mental Exercise
J38 Travel Information

1 In the news

Present perfect • Past simple

1 These pictures all accompany news stories. What do you think has happened in each case?

📼 Now listen to the news stories. For each story answer the questions.

  – What events are reported using the Present perfect tense?
  – What other details are given?

2 Think of something that's been in the news this week. Summarise the story in two or three sentences.

2 Tell me more

Questions

1 Look at this piece of news. What other details might you want
to know? Write some questions.

We've just had a baby

Is it a girl or a boy?

hospital?

name?

...?

When was it born?

first?

...?

Now look at the letter on page 121.
Did the writer answer your questions?

2 *a* On a piece of paper, write a sentence giving a piece of news about yourself or
someone you know. Exchange sentences with your partner.

b Look at your partner's sentence, and write some questions asking for more
details. Then give the paper back.

c Expand your sentence into a paragraph, adding the details your partner asked for.

3 What have you been doing?

Present perfect continuous & simple

> Well, this month I've been serving customers as one of the staff is ill. I've also been doing the accounts, writing letters, ordering new stock. And I've bought a new delivery van.

> Basically, I've been learning my lines. I suppose I've learnt about half of them now. I play an American, so I've also been taking lessons in American English.

> I've been doing all the usual things – driving around, visiting clients, giving out free samples. One thing I haven't done yet is fill in this month's expenses claim. I must do that.

1 *a* Read these texts. What do you think the people's jobs are?

b What is the difference between the Present perfect simple (*I've done*)
and the Present perfect continuous (*I've been doing*)?

2 Work in pairs. Find out whether your partner
has been doing any of these things recently.

– going out a lot   – spending a lot of money
– working hard   – watching TV a lot
– going to bed late   – travelling a lot

Example:
A Have you been going out a lot recently?
B Yes, I have. I've been out four times this week.
  No, I haven't. I've been painting my flat.
  No. I only went out once last week.

4 Eavesdropping

1 🖭 You will overhear a couple having an argument. Which of these sentences do you think are true?

> *a* The woman hasn't been sleeping well.
> *b* The man has found a job.
> *c* The woman hasn't been working very hard.
> *d* The man has been sitting around doing nothing.
> *e* They haven't been getting on well for some time.

2 🖭 You will overhear bits of three more conversations. What are the conversations about? Imagine what the people have (or haven't) been doing.

Grammar Checklist

Present perfect active & passive

Active: **have/has** + *past participle*

A prisoner **has** escaped.
They **haven't found** him yet.
Have you **heard** the news?

Passive: **have/has** + **been** + *past participle*

A new planet **has been** discovered.
He **hasn't been** arrested yet.
Have you **been** invited to the party?

Present perfect & Past simple tenses

Present perfect – *for announcing news of recent events (without saying when).*
Past simple – *for giving details.*

Five prisoners **have** escaped from Bedford Prison. They **broke** out late last night and **drove** away in a green van.

– I've **bought** a new coat.
– Really? How much **did** it **cost**?

Present perfect continuous & simple tenses

Present perfect continuous – *for talking about recent activities (how you have been spending your time).*

have/has + **been** + **-ing**

I've **been going** out a lot recently.
She's **been** preparing for her exams.
They **haven't been** speaking to each other.

Present perfect simple – *for talking about single complete events.*

I've **been** tidying my room. *(An activity)*
I've **tidied** my room. (= *I've finished it.*)

I've **been going** to the cinema a lot recently.
I've **seen** three films this week.

See also Reference section, page 137.

Focus on Form

1 Present perfect or past?

Fill the gaps with the correct form of the verbs in the box. Choose between the Present perfect simple and the Past simple.

be	go	see
decide	make	show
find	offer	tell

a Actress Lana Bernstein and her fourth husband .... to separate after only two months of marriage. They .... reporters yesterday that they both needed more time to follow their own careers.

b Great news! Nina .... a job at last. She .... for an interview last week, and they .... her the job straight away. It's only four days a week, but the pay's good. And we .... someone to look after the children, too.

c I've been having a great time since I came to Barcelona. I .... lots of new friends, and I .... out almost every night. Some friends of mine .... me round the town too, so I .... most of the sights already.

2 Present perfect active & passive

Example:

Last week's news   *This week's news*

Police are searching for three prisoners who escaped last night from Brixton prison. They

The three prisoners were back in Brixton prison today after being caught driving a stolen

A What's happened to those prisoners who escaped last week?
B They've been caught.

Student A: Look at last week's news on page 119, and ask B what's happened.

Student B: Look at today's news on page 120, and answer A's questions.

3 Present perfect continuous

Look at the pictures. What do you think the people have (or haven't) been doing?

Example: *Picture A*

He's been watching the late movie.
He hasn't been sleeping well.
He's been working very hard.

4 Recent activities & actions

1 What have these people been doing?
2 Add one more thing that each person has done (or hasn't done yet).

Example: *I've planted some vegetables and I've cut the grass.*

1 She's been working in the garden.
2 She hasn't watered the flowers yet.

a We've done some jigsaw puzzles and painted some pictures, but we haven't been to the playground yet.
b I've washed the vegetables and put the meat in the oven.
c I've bought some paper hats, but I haven't ordered the cake yet.
d We haven't seen Buckingham Palace yet, but we have been to all the big museums.
e I've paid the electricity bill and the rent.

5 Pronunciation

How do you say the words and phrases below?

a 've we've you've they've
   We've had a baby.
   We had a baby yesterday.

b The money has been found.
   The thieves have been arrested.

c Have you been working?
   What have you been doing?
   I've been watching TV.

Now listen and check your answers.

16 Teaching and learning

1 In the classroom

Morden Park Secondary Sc

Class:	Name:		
	Monday	Tuesday	We
9.00	ENGLISH		
9.45	GEOGRAPHY		
10.30	B R	E A	K
10.45	COMPUTER		
11.30	STUDIES		
12.15	L U	N C	H
1.30			
2.15			

1 *a* Look at the timetable. What other subjects would you expect to find on it?

  b 🔲 You will hear four people talking about subjects they were taught at school.

  What subject are they talking about? How do you know?

2 Work in groups. Choose a subject that you all studied (or are studying) at school. Think about these questions:

  – Did you enjoy it?
  – What was the teacher like?
  – What did you have to do?
  – What *didn't* you do?
  – Did you learn anything useful?

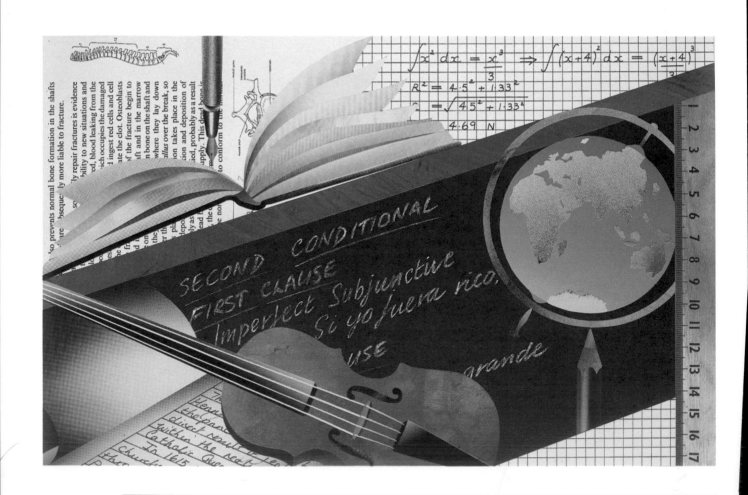

2 How to ...

1 Do you know how to do any of the things in the box? Complete the table. Add one other thing you know how to do.

windsurf	touch-type
bake bread	ride a horse
ski	shear a sheep
juggle	dance a waltz
read music	draw a bicycle

I don't know how to ...	
I know how to ... (but I'm not very good)	
I'm quite good at ...	
I'm very good at ...	

2 Choose one skill you would like to know more about. What would you like to know?

Now find someone who knows more about it than you, and find out as much as you can.

Did you find out what you wanted to know?

3 Going through the system

You will hear someone answering questions about the American education system.

1 Look at the questions in the box. Which questions does he answer?

    a At what age do children start
       primary school?
    b What about secondary school?
    c Are all subjects compulsory?
    d Do all students follow the same
       course?
    e What's the school leaving age?
    f What are the most important
       school exams?
    g How many subjects do they take?
    h How long does it take to get a
       university degree?

2 *Student A:* **Imagine you're an American.** Ask about the education system in B's country.

Student B: **Answer A's questions.**

4 Improve your memory

How many days?

In some cultures, people have no problem remembering which months have 31 days and which have 30. In Iran, for example, the first six months have 31 days, the next five have 30, and the last has 28 or 29. And in Thailand, you can tell from the names of the months: those with 31 days end in *-om* (e.g. January is *Magarakom*), those with 30 days end in *-on* (e.g. September is *Kanyayon*) and February ends in *-an: Kumpapan*.

Most countries, however, use some kind of mnemonic, or memory aid. In Britain, a rhyme is used:

> *30 days have September*
> *April, June and November.*
> *All the rest have 31*
> *Excepting February alone*
> *Which has but 28 days clear*
> *And 29 in each leap year.*

What about your country?

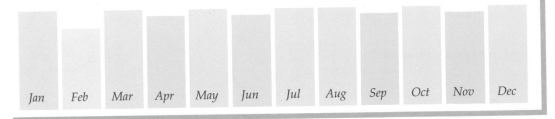

Jan Feb Mar Apr May Jun Jul Aug Sep Oct Nov Dec

READING

1 Look at the text called *How many days?*

   How do you remember which months have 31 days and which have 30?

2 Look at the text on the opposite page, and read about *one* of the two memory techniques.

   Then use the technique you have learned to test yourself.

LISTENING

You will hear someone describing a technique for learning new vocabulary in a foreign language.

1 How does the technique use
   - the learner's mother tongue?
   - a visual image?

2 Look at the four pictures. For each one, note down
   - the foreign word
   - its meaning in English
   - the 'help words' the speaker uses.

3 Choose one of the words from the two lists on the opposite page. How could you use this technique to help you learn it?

REMEMBERING THINGS IN THE RIGHT ORDER

Suppose you want to remember a sequence of ten unrelated items in a particular order. Here are two techniques that you can use.

Technique 1: Pegwords

First, you have to learn a set of pegwords, one for each of the numbers one to ten. Since each of these rhymes with its number, this is a fairly easy task. Try it for yourself:

One = *bun*	Five = *hive*	Eight = *gate*
Two = *shoe*	Six = *sticks*	Nine = *wine*
Three = *tree*	Seven = *heaven*	Ten = *hen*
Four = *door*		

Having mastered this, you are ready to go; suppose the ten words you are trying to remember are: *battleship, octopus, chair, sheep, castle, rug, grass, beach, milkmaid, binoculars.*

Take the first pegword, which is *bun* (rhyming with *one*), and imagine a picture of a bun interacting in some way with a battleship: you might for example imagine a battleship sailing into an enormous floating bun. Now take the second pegword, *shoe*, and imagine it interacting with *octopus*, perhaps a large shoe with an octopus sitting in it. Pegword nine is *wine*, and the ninth item is *milkmaid*, so you might imagine a milkmaid milking a cow and getting wine rather than

milk. And so on. Having created these pictures, you should be able to come up with an accurate list of the ten words in the right order.

Technique 2: Places

First of all, think of ten locations in your home, choosing them so that the sequence of moving from one to the other is an obvious one – for example, front door to entrance hall, to kitchen, to bedroom, and so on.

Check that you can imagine moving through your ten locations in the same order without difficulty.

Now think of ten items and imagine them in those locations. If the first item is *grass*, you might imagine opening your front door and wiping your feet on a doormat made of grass. If the second is a *cabbage*, you might imagine your hall blocked by an enormous cabbage. If item number three is *sheep*, you could imagine someone in the kitchen trying to put a whole sheep into the oven. And so on.

The locations need not, of course, be in your own home. They could be a typical trip along your high street or around your place of work or school.

Test yourself

Now try to create similarly memorable images for the ten items in either of these lists.

Then cover up the page, and see if you can write down the ten items in order.

If you haven't yet had time to learn the ten pegwords or locations by heart, write them down and use them to help you.

1	shirt	5	camera	8	handkerchief
2	eagle	6	mushroom	9	sausage
3	paper clip	7	crocodile	10	king
4	rose				

1	horse	5	watch	8	typewriter
2	bullet	6	window	9	jacket
3	table	7	ostrich	10	cloud
4	cigar				

Adapted from *Your Memory, A User's Guide* by Alan Baddeley.

1 Flashbacks

Past perfect tense

Sophie wandered aimlessly from room to room. The flat,

1

felt empty, too big for one person.

2

she wondered.

3

There was a heavy silence everywhere. She couldn't even put any music on.

4

She made herself a cup of coffee, and sat at the kitchen table, staring at the note with its familiar handwriting.

5   **6**

c/o Ewa Gradowska, ul. Smolna 30 m 21, 00–837 Warsaw, she read. No telephone number. She wondered who Ewa Gradowska was.

7   **8**

Not that it mattered, really. There would be no emergency, she was sure of that.

☐ 'Just in case there's an emergency,' he'd told her.	☐ which had once seemed so small,
☐ Had he known her for a long time? Years perhaps?	☐ Why had she let him leave so easily?
☐ Or had they only just met?	☐ He'd taken the cassette player. She'd agreed to that.
☐ He'd left his address in case she needed to get in touch.	☐ Why hadn't she asked him to wait and think again?

1 Fit the missing parts back into the story. What do they all have in common?

2 Now fill the gaps in the text below with suitable flashbacks.

At the top of the hill he stopped the car and looked down at the village where .... He saw the grey houses, the church, the park, the old schoolhouse where .... It was all exactly as he remembered it: the smoke drifting up from the paper factory; the old garage which had only one petrol pump; the hotel, with its bright yellow walls. And there, in the distance, was the farm. With a grin, he remembered the day, 20 years before, when ....

He drove down to the hotel and went into the bar to get some lunch. He sat at the table by the window, where .... Where was she now, he wondered. Was she still living here? Or ....?

2 Changes in the past

Past and Past perfect tenses

1 Read the description below, and say what the guests had (or hadn't) done.

As soon as I got home, I realised that it had been a mistake to let them use my flat.

– All the lights were on.
– The front door was open.
– There was no-one in the flat.
– There were cigarette burns in the carpet.
– There were piles of dirty dishes everywhere.
– There was no food in the fridge.
– The plants were all dead.

2 Choose one of these remarks. Imagine what things were like and what had happened.

a Clearly they were expecting some very important guests for dinner.
b When I saw her again, I didn't recognise her at first.
c After only one year in power, the government was already very unpopular.

3 Reporting

Reported speech and thought

1 What did these people actually say (or think)? Fill the bubbles.

They said they were police officers.

She said she would meet me at the airport.

After a time, she realised that someone was following her.

He told me he'd fought in the Vietnam War.

When I got to the station, I discovered that the train had already left.

The Prime Minister told reporters that he was not going to resign.

2 a Think of a time recently when one of these things happened to you:
   – you realised that something was wrong
   – someone told you a surprising piece of news
   – you met somebody interesting.

   Write a sentence about it using *said*, *told*, *discovered* or *realised*.

b Tell your partner what happened. Include your sentence in what you say.

4 The dead rabbit

🔊 **You will hear a story called** *The dead rabbit*. **The story is in five parts. Listen to each part of the story and answer the questions.**

Part 1
– What was the dog like?
– What had it done on previous occasions?

Part 2
– What did the dog bring home?
– What had it done?
– What do you think the man did next?

Part 3
– What hadn't the dog done?
– What do you think the man did next?

Part 4
– What did the man do?
– What happened the next morning?
– What do you think the neighbour said?

Part 5
– Why was the neighbour upset?
– What had the dog done?

Grammar Checklist

Past perfect tense

Active: **had(n't)** + *past participle – for going <u>back</u> from the past to events that happened earlier.*

The house was empty – everyone **had left.**
She **hadn't** changed – she looked just the same.
He showed me photos of the places he**'d** visited.

Passive: **had(n't) been** + *past participle*

They pulled down the buildings that **had been** destroyed in the fire.

Past & Past perfect tenses

There **was** some food on the table.
They**'d left** some food on the table.
Some food **had been left** on the table.

The door **wasn't** locked.
They **hadn't** locked the door.
The door **hadn't been** locked.

Reported speech & thought

Change the verb one tense further back:

Present	→	Past
will	→	would
Past Present perfect	→	Past perfect

He told me he **was** a tourist.
　　(His actual words: '**I'm** a tourist.')

She said she **would** teach me Japanese.
　　(She said '**I'll** teach you Japanese.')

I suddenly discovered that **I'd lost** my wallet.
　　(I thought '**I've lost** my wallet.')

See also Reference section, page 138.

Focus on Form

1 Which tense?

Put the verbs in brackets into the correct form. Use the Past simple (*did*), the Past continuous (*was doing*) or the Past perfect (*had done*).

The clock said 11.30. I (be) in the office for two hours, and the phone (not ring) once. Maybe I (be) in the wrong business.

I (put) my feet up on the desk, and (pick) up the morning paper. The New York Hurricanes (lose) again. The police (pull) two more bodies out of the river. Myra Halliday (just divorce) her sixth husband. Nothing new there. I (start) doing the crossword.

I (still do) the crossword when the door (open) and a man (come) in. He (be) tall, fairly good-looking, and in his mid-forties. He (wear) a white suit and a loud tie, and he (smoke) an expensive cigar. He (look) as if he (not sleep) for a week. I (see) him before. His picture (be) on the front page of the newspaper that I (hold) in my hand. He (be) Myra Halliday's latest ex-husband.

"Your boss in, honey?" he (ask).

"Where I come from, mister," I (say), "people knock before they open doors. And that's a No Smoking sign on the wall."

2 Explanations: the Past perfect

Student A: Read out the sentences below.

Student B: Give a suitable explanation from the box, using the Past perfect tense.

Example: *He had to go by bus …*

… because his car had broken down.

a He had to go by bus …
b He couldn't pay for the meal …
c His parents bought him a new bike …
d He was hungry …
e He knew a lot about the French Revolution …
f He couldn't get into the restaurant …
g He had to stay in after school …
h He couldn't get in touch with them …

> He didn't reserve a table.
> He passed his exam.
> He lost their address.
> His car broke down.
> He didn't have any breakfast.
> He didn't do his homework.
> He studied history at university.
> He left his wallet at home.

3 Reported speech

Work in pairs. Last weekend you were both invited to a rather smart party. You each spent some time talking to two different people.

Turn to page 119 (*Student A*) or page 120 (*Student B*) to find out what they said to you. Then try and remember what they said, and tell your partner, using reported speech.

Example: '*I'm a film actor. I've just come back from making a film in Hollywood.*'

He told me that he was a film actor, and that he'd just come back from making a film in Hollywood.

4 Pronunciation

How do you say the words and phrases below?

a The guests had arrived.
   Everyone had enjoyed themselves.
   The guests hadn't arrived.
   She hadn't been abroad.
b There was someone in the room.
   There were people everywhere.
c They said they were reporters.
   He told me we'd met before.
   She realised that she'd forgotten his name.

 Now listen and check your answers.

Breaking the law

1 Crime ...

A Customs officials found 5 kilos of heroin hidden inside the tyres of the car.

B The two gunmen left the shop with more than £10,000 worth of watches and jewellery.

C When he opened the door, she shot him three times in the chest. According to the pathologist's report he died instantly.

D She said she would publish the photos unless he gave her £5,000.

E A ransom of $1,500,000 dollars was demanded for the child's release.

F Shortly after take-off, they produced guns and forced the pilot to fly to Cyprus, where the plane was given permission to land, and surrounded by armed troops.

G When the school was reopened after the weekend, staff found that three classrooms had been completely wrecked: furniture and windows were broken, and graffiti had been sprayed on the walls.

H He broke into the flat at 3.00 in the morning and took £3,000 from a cupboard.

1 Look at the extracts from newspapers and match them with the crimes in the box.

blackmail	murder
burglary	robbery
hijacking	smuggling
kidnapping	vandalism

What do you call the *people* who commit these crimes?

2 *a* Choose a crime and think of a real incident that you know of.

b Work in groups. Decide which of your stories is the most interesting.

c Tell the story you have chosen to the rest of the class.

2 ... and punishment

1 What punishments would you give for the offences in the box?

Do you think the person should

- pay a fine?
- be sent to prison?
- be sentenced to death?
- be punished in some other way?
- not be punished at all?

shoplifting
dropping litter
spying for a foreign power
drunken driving
smoking marijuana
shooting a police officer
not paying income tax

2 In groups, compare your answers.

3 Guilty or not guilty?

1 Read the news story. What was Mr Cook charged with?

2 *a* What arguments do you think were used in court

  - by the prosecution?
  - by the defence?

b Which of these things do you think happened at the end of the trial?

  - Mr Cook was found not guilty.
  - He was found guilty and had to pay a fine.
  - He was found guilty and was sent to prison.

☐ Now listen to a news broadcast about the trial. What happened?

Passenger 'stabbed attacker on Tube with a swordstick'

A COMMUTER carrying a swordstick stabbed a man in the stomach after he tried to strangle him on a London Underground train, a court was told yesterday.

Mr Edward Cook drew his swordstick as he was held by the neck and his head was repeatedly struck against a door, it was said in Wood Green Crown Court.

The court heard that Mr Cook, aged 56, was returning home on the Victoria Line when two young men attacked him.

"One of them pushed him against the door of the carriage, holding him by the neck and banging him against the door. At that stage he took out his sword and used it on the person attacking him," Mr Michael Lawson, for the prosecution, told the jury.

The attacker, who smelled strongly of alcohol, was taken to hospital and treated for the wound. Mr Cook was arrested and charged with possessing an offensive weapon. He told police he carried the swordstick for self-defence while walking in Epping Forest. Mr Lawson said there was no lasting injury to the attacker.

After the incident Mr Cook was interviewed by police and explained why he used the swordstick.

Mr Cook yesterday

He said: "I did it as a last means of self-defence. It was a desperate act as my life was in danger."

The walking stick, which unscrewed to reveal a three-foot long blade and cost Mr Cook £400, was shown to the jury.

The case continues today.

4 Detective Shadow

LISTENING

You will hear two people playing a game in which one person reads out a murder mystery and the other person tries to solve it.

There are three characters:
- Uncle Cecil (the murder victim)
- Harry Fox (his nephew)
- Detective Shadow.

1 🔲 Listen to the first part of the recording and answer the questions.

  - What did Shadow see when he arrived?
  - What happened, according to Harry Fox?
  - What happened after Shadow arrived?

2 How does Shadow know that Harry Fox is lying?

  🔲 Now listen to the solution. Were you right?

READING

Here are four more crimes solved by Detective Shadow. What are the solutions?

1

Shadow opened the door to Dr Adam Apple's office and looked around him. Dr Apple's head lay on his desk surrounded by a pool of blood. On the floor to his right lay a small handgun. There were powder burns on his right temple, indicating that he had been shot at close range. On his desk was a suicide note, and his right hand held the pen that had written it. Shadow recorded the time as 3.30 pm, and ascertained that death had occurred within the past hour. As Shadow was gathering clues, Dr Apple's wife burst into the office and screamed, "Good lord, my husband's been shot!" She ran toward him, saw the note and cried, "Why would he want to kill himself?"

"This was no suicide" said Shadow. "This was clearly a case of murder." How does he know?

2

"I have the only key to the room containing the jewellery of my late aunt Maggy," said Sid Crook. "Since her death a week ago, neither I nor anybody else has entered this room. I was quite pleased to hear all her jewellery was to be sold and the proceeds to go to charity," continued Crook.

Shadow removed a huge plant whose broad leaves were turned towards the wall, partially covering the safe. While Crook was opening the combination lock, Shadow crossed the room to sit on the ledge of the large bay window. Crook opened the safe, and removed the bag of jewels. "I'm sure these jewels will fetch a fortune for charity," said a smiling Sid Crook. "I'll bet these jewels are either fake or there are a few missing," replied Shadow. What made Shadow suspicious?

3

"Mr Grey?" inquired Shadow, "I'm afraid I have some bad news for you. Your brother-in-law is dead and I have reason to believe he was murdered."

"Oh no!" replied Grey. "I just saw Sam a couple of days ago. To tell you the truth though, I'm not surprised. Sam did have a big mouth and quite a few enemies. As a matter of fact both of my sisters' husbands and Sam had a big fight over a business deal that went wrong. Then there was a friend of my brother's who lent Sam a lot of money and never got it back. Another person is my wife's brother who just got out of jail. He accused Sam of framing him. He swore he would get even." As Grey talked on about Sam's enemies, Shadow got out the handcuffs and arrested him on suspicion of murder. Why?

4

Jim Cool waited until Ed Fry left the office of author Harry Queen. Cool slipped on a pair of gloves, took a handgun from his desk, and crossed the hall to Queen's office. As Queen looked up to see who was there, Cool took aim and shot. Cool dropped the gun on the floor, picked up the telephone on Queen's desk and called the police. He then went back across the hall to his own office and hid the gloves. Shadow arrived moments later and Cool told his story. "I was working at my desk when I heard a shot. I ran to the hall and saw a man fitting the description of Ed Fry running from Queen's office. I went to Queen's office and found him lying on the floor dead. I immediately picked up the phone on Queen's desk and called the police."

Several hours later Shadow arrested Cool for murder. Why was he so easily caught?

All five cases are adapted from *MindTrap* ©, under license to Spears Games ®.

Review: Units 13–18

Find out

1 A Which person in your family are you closest to in age? Tell B who it is.

B Find out how different A is from the person he/she has chosen. Ask about
  - appearance   – personality
  - interests   – abilities.

2 Find out from other students what kinds of TV programmes they enjoy and don't enjoy watching.

Who do you have most in common with?

3 In groups, talk about what you've been doing recently. Find out
  – who's been enjoying themselves the most
  – who's been the busiest.

Role-play

MILLIONAIRE FOUND MURDERED AT COUNTRY RESIDENCE

A You're the housekeeper. You discovered the body this morning. What did you find? How had the victim been murdered?

B You're the dead man's secretary. You spent yesterday working with him. Who else was there? Did anything unusual happen?

C You're the police officer investigating the case. What have you found out so far? Do you suspect anyone?

D You're a journalist. Think of questions to ask A, B and C.

Then interview A, B and C. Report what they said to the rest of the class.

Conversational English

1 Giving advice

1 Look at the pictures above. What problems do the people have? Which bubble should go with which picture?

2 What advice would you give the person below?

My husband's father came to live with us after his wife died while he looked for somewhere else to live. This was six months ago, and he's still here. I feel sorry for him, but he's quite difficult, and he does nothing to help around the flat. I want him to go, but my husband seems to like having him around.

Now think of a problem of your own and ask different people for some advice. What was the best (and worst) advice you received?

Talking points

Choose one of these topics. Take it in turns to say a sentence or two about it.

Two towns in your country. How are they different?

Radio stations

Today's news

'I'd like to be good at ...'

What's wrong with the education system

'Do you know the joke about ...?'

'When I was a child, I believed ...'

Smuggling

Words

1 **What are/were**
   - your best three subjects at school?
   - your worst three subjects at school?

2 **Add words to these lists.**
   - foreign news, advertisements ...
   - primary school, secondary school ...
   - burglar, murderer ...

3 **Answer these questions.**
   - Where would you find a *headline*?
   - What happens in a *chat show*?
   - Have you ever learnt anything *by heart*?
   - What's the penalty in your country for *shoplifting*?
   - What does a *jury* do?

2 Making choices

1 ▭ You will hear four short conversations in which people make choices.

   a What is going on in each conversation?

   b How do the speakers use the expressions in the box?

> I'll ...
> I'd like ...
> I'd rather ...
> I'd prefer ...

2 Look at these situations.
   How do you think the people might use the expressions in the box?

Situation 1

Student A: Your boss B is going abroad on a business trip. You have to arrange travel and hotel accommodation. Find out what he/she wants to do.

Student B: Decide how and when you want to travel and what kind of hotel and hotel room you'd like.

Situation 2

Student A: You want to go to an exhibition which is only open today and tomorrow. You'd like A to come with you.

Student B: There's a good film on TV, and you're feeling tired. You're not busy tomorrow.

Now choose one of the situations and act out a conversation.

Situation 3

A & B: You're in a restaurant. Look at the menu and decide what to order.

STARTERS

Tomato soup   Melon
Pâté with toast and butter   Deep-fried mushrooms

MAIN COURSES

Salmon in cream sauce with seasonal vegetables
Cheeseburger with French fries and mayonnaise
Mushroom omelette with mixed salad
Chicken and prawn with black bean sauce & noodles
Lamb curry (medium hot) with boiled rice and salad

SWEETS

Fresh fruit salad
American apple pie with ice-cream
Death-by-chocolate gateau, served with cream

DRINKS

Mineral water   Cola   Red wine   Coffee
Fruit juice   Beer   White wine   Tea

1 Favourite things

Present perfect + for/since

1 Read these extracts from a magazine article.

a Which objects is the woman describing?

b How long has she had each one?
Complete these sentences.
– She's had it for …
– She's had it since …

Favourite things

Novelist Jo Hamilton, 26, takes us on a guided tour of her favourite possessions

66 I bought this ▮▮▮
while I was travelling in
Southern Morocco about eight
years ago. It's very precious to me
because I had very little money at
the time and I spent a whole day
bargaining to get it at a good
price. I used to have it on the
floor, but it started to get a bit
worn, so now it hangs on
the wall of my living room. **99**

66 This was always my
favourite ▮▮▮
when I was a child – I was
given it for my third birthday,
and for years I used to take it
everywhere with me. These
days I keep it in my bedroom,
and even after all this time it's
very comforting to know it's
there keeping an eye on
me while I'm asleep. **99**

66 This ▮▮▮ used to
be my grandmother's – my
grandfather gave it to her when
they got engaged. She gave it to me
when I got married five years ago,
and asked me to pass it on to my
own grandchildren, which is just
what I intend to do. It's not worth
very much, but I think it's beautiful, and I only wear it on
very special occasions. **99**

2 *Student A:* Write a sentence describing one of your favourite possessions. Don't say how
long you've had it or where you got it. Give your sentence to B.

Student B: Imagine how long A has had the thing, and why it is important to him/her.
Make some notes.

Now tell A what you thought. How far were you from the truth?

2 Then and now

1 Write the missing sentences in the table.

	How long ago …?	*How long …?*
a	She started playing the trumpet two years ago.	She's been playing the trumpet for two years.
b	....	I've been a member of Greenpeace for six months.
c	....	Estonia has been independent since 1990.
d	They met in 1954.	....
e	They came to stay with us three days ago.	....
f	....	He's been working here since he left school.
g	I opened this bank account when I went to college.	....
h	Mozart died more than 200 years ago.	....
i	....	He's been playing professional football for 10 years.

2 Write three true sentences about yourself. Choose verbs from the box.

start   live   be
play   join   meet

3 It's a long time since …

1 You will hear three people talking about things they haven't done for a long time.

a Listen and complete the table.

	Activity	*When did they last do it?*	*Why did they stop?*
1			
2			
3			

b The speakers use three different structures to say when they last did things. What are they?

2 Work in groups.

Think of something you used to enjoy doing that you haven't done for a long time. Tell the others about it, and answer any questions they may have.

4 Guess how long ...

1 'We're just celebrating our diamond wedding anniversary.'

How long have they been married?

2 *a* How long is it since the Big Bang?
   b How old is the Earth?

   c How long have dinosaurs been extinct?
   d How long ago did *homo sapiens* appear?

3 What's wrong with these statements?

   a 'My grandfather's had the same biro since 1935.'
   b 'Shakespeare drank tea constantly while he was writing his plays.'

c 'I've just bought a new Citröen 2CV.'

4 How long have these countries been independent?
   a The United States of America.
   b India.
   c Latvia.

5 How long ago ...
   a ... was the Great Pyramid built?

   b ... did the Beatles have their first No.1 hit?

   c ... did Mao Tse-tung die?

---

1 Work in groups. Do you know the answers to these questions?
If you don't know an answer, make a guess.

Now listen to the answers. The group with the nearest answer scores one point.
Who won?

2 Now make up two more questions, and see if other groups can answer them.

Grammar Checklist

Present perfect continuous tense

have/has been + -ing – *for talking about activities that started in the past and are still going on.*
He**'s been** trying to phone her for three hours.
   (*not* he's trying)
They**'ve been** going out together since June.

Stative verbs

be, have (= *possess*), **know**
No continuous form – use Present perfect simple.
I**'ve had** these jeans for five years.
She**'s been** away for nearly a month.

for & since

I've known them **for** years.
I've known them **since** 1975.
I've known them **since** we first moved here.

How long ...? & How long ago ...?

How long + *Present perfect continuous or simple*
– **How long** has she been working here?
– For three months.
– **How long** have you been in this flat?
– Since June.

How long ago (*or* **When**) + *Past tense*
– **How long ago** did she start working here?
– Three months ago.
– **When** did you move into this flat?
– In June.

Negative duration structures

I **haven't ridden** a bike since I was a child.
It's ages **since** I (**last**) rode a bike.
The last time I rode a bike was in 1982.

See also Reference section, page 139.

Focus on Form

1 For & since

Complete these sentences about yourself
(1) using *for* (2) using *since*.

Example: *I've had this watch …*

… for six months.
… since October.
… since my last birthday.

a I've been in this room …
b I've been learning English …
c I've had these shoes …
d I've had this coursebook …
e I've been at this school …

2 Since when?

Student A: Choose one of the events in the box
and imagine what things have been like since
then.

Student B: Can you guess which item A was
thinking of? Complete each sentence using an
item from the box.

Examples:

A He's been eating in expensive restaurants …
B … ever since he won the lottery.

A He's been depressed …
B … ever since his girlfriend left him.

… (ever) since	he left school.
	he won the lottery.
	he visited the USA.
	his girlfriend left him.
	he lost all his money.
	he crashed his car.
	he came out of hospital.

3 How long …? & How long ago …?

Ask your partner these questions. If the answer is
'Yes', ask a question with *How long …?* or *How
long ago …?*

Example:

A Do you do anything to keep fit?
B Yes. I play basketball.
A | How long have you been playing?
      | How long ago did you start playing?

4 Negative duration

Add a sentence to these remarks, saying how long
it is since something happened.

Example: *I'm starving …*

I haven't eaten since breakfast.
I haven't eaten for six hours.
It's six hours since I had anything to eat.

a I'd love to visit Berlin again …
b I don't think she likes me any more …
c I'm afraid my Spanish is rather rusty …
d It's no good asking me what's on at the
     cinema …
e He's the laziest person I know …

5 Pronunciation

How do you say the words and phrases below?

a He's been trying to phone you.
     They've been talking for hours.

b How long have you known him?
     How long has she been waiting?
     How long have they been talking?

c I haven't been there for years.
     He hasn't been out since the weekend.

▭ **Now listen and check your answers.**

Do you know anyone who comes from a different country?

Have you got a pet?

Have you got a bike/motorbike/car/boat?

Do you do anything to keep fit?

Do you play any board games?

Do you have any relatives living abroad?

20 In your lifetime

1 Birth, marriage and death

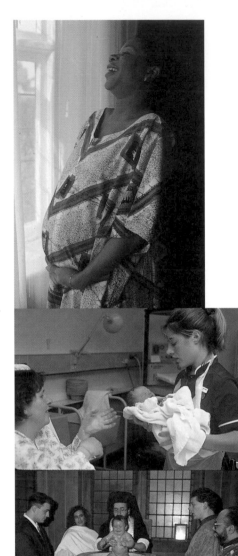

1 What vocabulary do you associate with birth, marriage and death?
Write a list of words for each group of pictures.

2 You will hear five people describing birth, marriage and death customs in different parts of the world. Here are some of the things they talk about:

silver	money	eating and drinking
a white dress	sweets	dancing
chopsticks	flowers	songs

Which do you expect to be about birth, which about marriage and which about death?

🔲 Now listen to the recording.

Think of birth, marriage and death customs in your own country.
Which do you think a foreigner would find the most unusual?

2 Age groups

Childhood
Adolescence
Young adulthood
Middle age
Old age

1 Look at these age groups. At what age do you think you move from one to another?

2 Look at the adjectives. Do you think they apply to any particular age group?

Think of some other adjectives that could go with each age group.

helpless   ambitious   rebellious

self-conscious   naughty   shy

wise   lonely   independent

3 Legal age

Age and the law: some facts about Britain

School-leaving age
Children have to stay at school until the age of 16. There is no upper age limit.

Alcohol
You have to be 18 to buy alcohol in a shop or a pub, but if you're 16 and you're having a meal in a pub, you can drink beer or wine with it.

Prosecution
In Scotland, you can be prosecuted for a crime at the age of 8. In England and Wales, the age is 10. You can't be sent to prison until you're 21.

Motor vehicles
16-year-olds can ride a motorbike of up to 50 cc. At 17 you can ride any bike or drive a car.

Smoking
You can smoke cigarettes at any age, but you can't go into a shop and buy them until you are 16.

Armed forces
Men can join the army at 16, women at 17. If you're under 18, you need your parents' consent.

Marriage
You can get married at 16 with your parents' consent. Otherwise you have to wait till you're 18.

Paid employment
You can take a part-time job at 13, and a full-time job at 16 (i.e. when you've left school).

Voting
Anyone aged 18 or over can vote in a general election.

Retirement age
Women can retire on full pension at 60. Men have to wait till they're 65.

Entering Parliament
The minimum age for becoming a Member of Parliament is 21. The youngest person to become an MP in the 20th century was Bernadette Devlin, who was elected a week before her 22nd birthday.

Read the text about British law.

What do *you* think should be the legal age for these activities? Fill in the table.

Compare your answers with your partner's.

Leaving school		Joining the army	
Drinking alcohol		Getting married	
Being prosecuted		Getting a job	
Riding a motorbike		Voting	
Driving a car		Retirement	
Smoking		Entering Parliament	

4 A Good Boy, Griffith

READING

Read each section of the story in turn and answer the questions.

Section 1
What can you tell about
– Griffith?
– Blodwen?
– Morgan?

Section 2
What else do you now know about the three characters?

Section 3

| Griffith gave a ring to Gwen ... | → | ... He wants to give the ring to Gwen again. |

What happened in between?

Section 4
What is Griffith's problem?

DISCUSSION

What do you think will happen next? Imagine an ending to the story.

LISTENING

You will hear the last two sections of the story.

Section 5
Does Griffith bring the money?
Does Blodwen give him the ring?
What does Blodwen promise?

Section 6
'Blodwen felt her heart capsize.' Why?
What does Morgan think happened?
What actually happened?

A GOOD BOY, GRIFFITH

by Leslie Thomas

1   GRIFFITH came over the hill behind the pit and turned the bend in the lane to the red brick cottage. It was too early for Morgan to be home from the garage yet, he knew that. Blodwen would be alone. Walking up to the gate he noticed how the windows shone clean in the late afternoon sun. Just like her, of course; always neat and decent. Never a speck of dust, never a thing out of place. She might have been his wife, but it was a good job she wasn't. He would never have been able to keep things the way she wanted them.

2   She came to the door almost immediately.

Griffith shyly reached for his cap. 'Hello Blod,' he said. 'Hope you don't mind me ...'

'What d'you want, Griffith?' she asked suspiciously. 'It's not decent for you to be calling on me, you know. Not now I'm wed; an' people knowing how we were an' all. What d'you want?'

'Well, let me come in and I'll tell you, girl. Don't keep me out here.'

For a moment she was undecided. Then she opened the door wider and he went into the living room. 'Just as I thought,' he mused. 'Not a plate out of place. Poor old Morgan. A good man, too.'

He looked at her, wondering if this could be the same girl he had asked to marry him on the night of the Institute dance. He realised now what a narrow escape he had had.

3   'Blod,' he said determinedly. 'I've come about the ring.'

A look of slow, smug triumph settled across her face. 'I thought you might,' she said. 'What about it? If you think you're getting it back, think again.'

He paled a little. 'Look, Blod,' he pleaded, 'it's important right now. Anyway, Morgan's given you a tidy little ring. Much better that one is.'

'Who do you want it for this time?' she said craftily. 'Seems that ring's been around a bit already.'

He told her that Gwen had come back.

'You know Gwen,' he said encouragingly.

She laughed, a mean little laugh with no laughter in it. 'Oh, Griffith. You're going round in circles. She was the one before me.'

And the only one, thought Griffith. You caught me on the rebound. Now she has come back from Cardiff, and she is going to stay, and she says it was all her fault, and she wants to start again.

4   'But why do you want the ring, Griff? Jenkins in the High Street has plenty in the window.'

Griffith lost his temper. He went red about the roots of his black hair, and he banged his fist down so that the table shook and it scared her. 'Listen, Blod,' he said. 'I want that ring. I'll pay you. She doesn't know I gave it to you. She wants the same one.'

'Then it's fifty pounds, Griffith,' she said abruptly.

He gasped: 'Fifty! Don't be daft, Blod. It's not worth ten.'

'Fifty,' she repeated firmly.

'But I haven't got that much and I couldn't get it. Talk sense, girl.'

'There's some lovely dresses in Cardiff, Griff. Saw them in the paper. Morgan's taking me down in the car on Tuesday ...'

He went out and slammed the door after him.

*   *   *

The next afternoon he went up the hill to the red

21 Finding out

1 Information questions

Question forms

1 Look at the answers in the bubbles.
  What do you think the questions were?

2 Write down three 'answers' about yourself, and show them to
  your partner. Can he/she guess what the questions are?

2 I'm not sure …

Indirect question forms

A	B
Who is she going out with?	I wonder who she's going out with.
How much money do I owe you?	I can't remember how much money I owe you.
How long is the Amazon?	I've no idea how long the Amazon is.
Have you met before?	I'm not sure whether you've met before.
When did they arrive?	Can you tell me when they arrived?
Has the train left yet?	Do you know if the train's left yet?

1 *a* **What's the difference between the sentences in Column A and those in Column B?**

   b **Combine these sentences to make indirect questions.**
   – Will they come to the party? I wonder.
   – How long has he been asleep? I'm not sure.
   – When does the concert begin? I don't know.
   – Have I read that book? I'm not sure.
   – What's 'car' in Spanish? Do you know?
   – What was I looking for? I can't remember.

2 **Write some true sentences beginning:**

   I wonder …   I'm not sure …

   I don't know …   I can't remember …

3 Getting to know you

Reported question forms

I was in the students' room waiting for my class to begin when the girl in the next seat asked me which class I was in …

I was sitting in a corner when a guy came up and asked me if I knew anyone at the party. I said I didn't …

I was waiting for my bus yesterday when a woman came and stood next to me and asked me how long I'd been waiting …

1 *a* **Read the texts. What do you think were the actual questions?**

   b 🔊 **Now listen to the scenes, and report the other questions.**

2 **In pairs, choose one of the situations above, and improvise a short conversation.**

   Student A: **You want to get to know B. Think of one or two questions you might ask to get a conversation going.**

   Student B: **Respond in any way you want.**

   Now report your conversation to the class.

4 Tags

1 Add the missing question tags to these remarks.

   [cassette icon] Now listen to the same remarks. In which ones

   – does the speaker really want to find out something?
   – is the speaker just expressing an opinion or belief?

2 What question tags might you use in these situations?

   – You've just seen someone you think you recognise.
   – You're driving to the airport to go on holiday.
   – Your dinner guests have just left.
   – You've just seen a Charlie Chaplin film.

   Choose one of the situations and improvise a short conversation.

Grammar Checklist

Wh- questions

What kind of coffee do you like?
What make is your cooker?
What happened to your coat?

How long did it take to get there?
How much does the suitcase weigh?

Whose coat is this? (*not* ~~Who's~~)

Indirect questions

Wh- *word + normal word order*
I don't know **what** his name **is**.
   (*not* ... ~~what is his name~~)
I wonder **where** they **went**.
Can you tell me **when** he's coming back?

if/whether + *normal word order*
I can't remember **if** I **posted** the letter.
   (*not* ... ~~did I post~~ ...)
Do you know **whether** Mr Smith **lives** here?

Reported questions

Wh- *word or* **if/whether** + *normal word order.*
Verb tense changes as in reported speech. (See Unit 17.)

'Do you know many people?' he asked.
→ He asked me **if I knew** many people.

'Where are you going?' she asked.
→ She asked him **where** he **was going**.

Question tags

They **live** here, **don't** they?
You **phoned** him, **didn't** you?
He's very talkative, **isn't** he?
You **can** drive, **can't** you?

She **doesn't** like fish, **does** she?
They **haven't** forgotten, **have** they?

See also Reference section, page 140.

Focus on Form

1 Questions with How ...?

How	How long	How much
How far	How many	How often

Fill the gaps with expressions from the box.

a .... children have you got?
b .... did you get here? On foot?
c .... is it from Rome to Pisa?
d .... did it cost?
e .... expensive was it?
f .... does it take you to get to work?
g .... does the ferry go? Once or twice a day?
h .... have you known them?
i .... sugar do you take?
j .... high is Mount Everest?

Now write three questions of your own.

2 Questions with What ...?

Make questions with *What ...?* plus an item from each box.

kind of	flavour
sort of	colour
type of	size
make of	

soup	music
flowers	crisps
curtains	car
shoes	T-shirt

Examples:

What sort of shoes should I wear?
What size curtains do we need?
What colour T-shirt did you get?

3 Quiz: indirect questions

Ask your partner questions beginning *Do you know ...?*

Examples:

When is St Valentine's Day?
Do you know when St Valentine's Day is?

Are spiders insects?
Do you know if spiders are insects?

a When is St Valentine's Day?
b Are spiders insects?
c How many days are there in a fortnight?
d Why can't you swim in the Sea of Tranquillity?
e What nationality was Christopher Columbus?
f When did he discover America?
g Is Denmark a monarchy?
h What is a *didgeridoo*?
i Where does Batman live?

4 Reported questions

Are you on a business trip?

Have you ever done this sort of work before?

Where does it hurt?

Have you been taking anything for the pain?

How long are you planning to stay?

When will you be able to start?

When did the trouble start?

Can you speak Spanish?

Report the questions you think were asked

a at a job interview
b at the doctor's
c going through customs.

Example:

The doctor asked me where it hurt ...

5 Checking: question tags

Decide whether you think these statements are true of your partner. Check by asking question tags.

Example: *You like spicy food.*

You like spicy food, don't you?   *or*
You don't like spicy food, do you?

a You like spicy food.
b You were born in this country.
c You can say 'Thank you' in Arabic.
d You've had measles.
e You believe in ghosts.
f You're left-handed.
g You know how to ski.

6 Pronunciation

How do you say the words and phrases below?

a What kind of biscuits do you want?
   What flavour ice-cream is that?
   What colour is his shirt?

b I wonder what they're doing.
   I'm not sure if we've met.

c He asked me if I spoke Japanese.

d You're not going, are you?
   (*I really want to know.*)

   You're not going, are you?
   (*I'm just checking.*)

  Now listen and check your answers.

1 Feelings

1 **How might you feel in these situations? Choose the best words from the box.**

a You're sitting chatting to friends after a good meal.
b Somebody has slashed the tyres on your car.
c You're introducing someone to a friend and you get his name wrong.
d It's your sixth birthday tomorrow.
e Your best friend is much more popular than you are.
f You're about to make a speech in public for the first time.
g You're alone in a house at night and you hear a window being opened downstairs.
h You've lost your wedding ring.
i Your neighbour keeps coming round and asking to borrow things.
j All the news in the papers seems to be about wars and disasters.
k You've heard a rumour that the factory where you work is going to close down.

angry
annoyed
depressed
embarrassed
excited
frightened
jealous
nervous
relaxed
upset
worried

2 **What makes you angry? depressed? jealous? …?**
Choose three feelings and write down a situation for each.

Find out if other students would feel the same.

2 Reactions

1 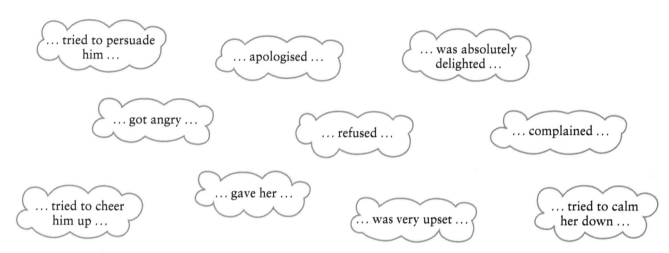 You will hear five short scenes. For each one,
find two expressions that describe what happened.

Now listen again, and say what happened in more detail.

... tried to persuade him ...

... apologised ...

... was absolutely delighted ...

... got angry ...

... refused ...

... complained ...

... tried to cheer him up ...

... gave her ...

... was very upset ...

... tried to calm her down ...

2 Work in pairs. Choose any two of the expressions and
prepare a short scene of your own.

3 Reviews

1 Look at the words in the box.

  a Which of them are positive and which are
  negative?

  b Which adjectives would fit in these
  sentences?

  – It was very ....
  – It was absolutely ....

amusing	awful
boring	brilliant
disappointing	dreadful
dull	fascinating
enjoyable	terrible
entertaining	terrific
exciting	wonderful
interesting	

2 *a* Look at these extracts from reviews.
   What do you think they're about?

It was a terrific match. Hodges is one of the most exciting players I've seen for ages.

The plot was entertaining enough, but I wish the author hadn't included all those long, boring descriptions of southern England.

This was a complete waste of an evening. The script was awful, the acting was wooden, and the camerawork was dreadful.

  b Choose something that several of you have
  seen or read recently, and write a short review.

  Now find out if other people agreed with you.

4 What's in a smile

READING

1 **Before you read:**

a Which of these smiles do you think are real? Which are false? How can you tell?

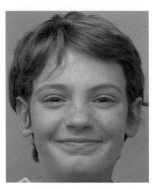

b Look at these faces. Which smile do you find the most attractive, and which the least attractive? Why?

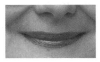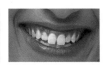

2 **Read the magazine article and find the answers to these questions.**

a Do people smile in every culture in the world?
b How many facial muscles do you use to smile?
c What happens to your blood pressure when you smile?
d What's the difference between a false smile and a real smile?
e How did Norman Cousins cure himself?
f Where can you find 'laughter rooms' and what are they for?
g Why did Aristotle Onassis wear dark glasses?
h What does a professional laugher do?

3 Note down any points in the article that you disagree with or find hard to accept. Compare notes with your partner.

Robert Holden, whose handbook *Laughter, The Best Medicine?* will be published early next year, runs the only NHS Laughter Clinic in Britain. Holden believes that laughter and smiling can not only heal the mind but the body as well.

LISTENING

1 Read the text about the Laughter Clinic. What kind of activities do you imagine take place there?

2 🔲 You will hear someone describing a typical session at the Clinic.

Make a list of all the activities she mentions.

Now compare your list with your partner's. Did you have the same answers?

What's in a *smile*

Smiling is ...

😊 **universal**. In his travels, Charles Darwin discovered that smiling was the only facial expression which was recognised instantly all over the world.

😊 **easy to see**. It is possible to recognise a smile on someone's face at a distance of 45 metres. You'd have to be much closer to decide whether the person was showing surprise, anger or fear.

😊 **simple**. You only use one facial muscle to smile. This is the zygomatic major muscle, which reaches down from the cheekbone to the corners of the lips. To look sad or angry, you need to use at least two muscles.

😊 **good for you**. Studies in the USA have shown that when you smile your heart rate slows down, your blood pressure goes down and the body begins to relax. This happens whether you are feeling happy or not. In fact, if you're feeling unhappy, the simple act of smiling is the first step to feeling better.

😊 **attractive**. According to American dentists Melvin and Elaine Denholtz, an attractive smile should show most of the upper teeth, at least two thirds of the length, and just the tips of the lower teeth.

Real smiles and false smiles

When you smile a real smile, two things happen to your face: your lips move up towards your cheeks, and your cheeks themselves go up and gather in the skin around the eyes. And a real smile will usually only last for up to four seconds.

False smiles are seen on the faces of politicians who have just lost an election, people who are pretending they're pleased to see you, and door-to-door salesmen. False smiles usually appear slightly too early or too late, and they tend to go on for too long.

But if you really want to know if a smile is real or false, look at the eyes. In a false smile these don't change – however much the person has practised smiling.

Eyes are important in other ways, too. When you feel good, your pupils get larger; when you feel bad, they become small. Ancient Chinese traders always looked their customers straight in the eye. If the pupils became big, the person was interested, and they could ask for more money.

DARK GLASSES
One reason why shipping tycoon Aristotle Onassis always wore dark glasses may have been so that his eyes would not give him away during delicate business negotiations.

Laughter: the best medicine

In 1964 an American journalist called Norman Cousins developed a serious problem with his back. It turned out that he had an illness called ankylosing spondylitis, which was extremely painful and, according to doctors, incurable. He was admitted to hospital, unable to move, and prescribed a course of strong pain-killing drugs. Cousins knew that negative emotions could make you ill, and began to wonder whether positive emotions – and particularly laughter – might make you better.

He stopped taking the drugs, and moved out of the hospital into a hotel room, which was not only a more cheerful place to be but was also much cheaper. There he hired a lot of Marx Brothers and *Candid Camera* films, and started to watch them. He found that every time he laughed, the laughter acted as an anaesthetic and gave him relief from pain. And the effect lasted some time: 10 minutes' laughter could give him around two hours free from pain.

More important, he found that he was slowly getting better, and eventually recovered completely from the illness.

For many years, the medical profession refused to take Cousins' claims seriously, but now things are changing and some American hospitals have set up 'laughter rooms', where patients can watch videos, listen to cassettes and read joke books, instead of sitting around feeling depressed.

LAUGHING FOR MONEY
A Frenchwoman, Julie Hette, works as a professional laugher. For a fee, she will come and laugh non-stop for you. Her record is 90 minutes. She guarantees that you will soon be laughing with her – even though you might not know what you're laughing about.

23 The unreal past

1 Dilemmas

would have done

On 13 October 1972 a plane carrying 45 passengers and crew bound for Santiago, Chile, crashed in a remote part of the High Andes. After waiting several days, the 27 survivors of the crash realised that they had no chance of being rescued. They were stranded high in the mountains above the snow line, and although they could shelter from the worst of the cold inside the plane, they had nothing to eat except snacks and chocolates that the plane had been carrying. These soon ran out, and they were faced with starvation. Then one of the survivors suggested that there was just one chance of survival: they could eat the flesh of the passengers that had died in the crash ...

1 a Read the story about the crash in the Andes. What was the dilemma facing the survivors?

Imagine you were one of the survivors. What would you have done?

b ▭ You will hear three people saying what they would have done in the situation.

Which speaker's opinion is closest to your own?

2 Work in groups. Look at one of these other dilemmas. What would you have done?

When the nine-year-old daughter of Ernest and Regina Twigg died in 1988, the post-mortem examination showed that she was not in fact their daughter. They made enquiries, and discovered that someone had made a mistake at the hospital where Mrs Twigg had had her baby girl: their daughter had been given to another couple, and the Twiggs had been given the other couple's baby. Their daughter, they learnt, was living with her 'family' in another part of the USA, 1,500 kilometres away ...

In August 1991, Dr Nigel Cox was treating a 70-year-old woman who was extremely ill with rheumatoid arthritis, and in constant pain. There was no chance that she would ever leave her bed again. The only way Dr Cox could relieve her pain was by giving her large doses of heroin. After a time, however, heroin was not enough to stop the pain, and the woman begged Dr Cox to give her a drug that would kill her ...

2 If ...

1 Look at the remarks above. What are the speakers talking about? What happened (or didn't happen)?

2 Write *If* ... sentences based on the remarks below.

Why didn't you tell me you were ill?

Sorry. I didn't know it was your birthday.

It's a pity the weather was so bad.

It's a good thing they didn't open my suitcase.

I didn't have any money with me.

3 A better place

2nd & 3rd conditionals

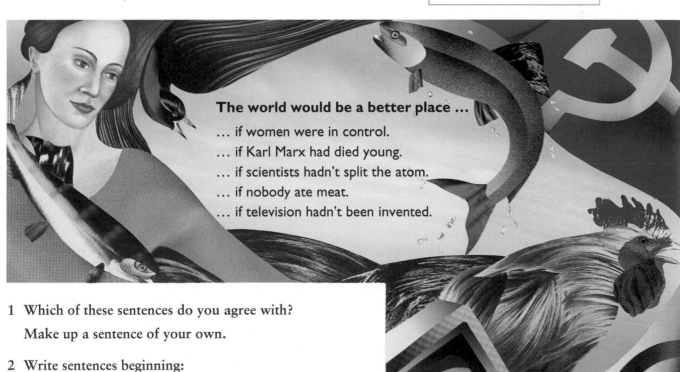

The world would be a better place ...

... if women were in control.

... if Karl Marx had died young.

... if scientists hadn't split the atom.

... if nobody ate meat.

... if television hadn't been invented.

1 Which of these sentences do you agree with?

Make up a sentence of your own.

2 Write sentences beginning:
   – This country would be a better place if ...
   – This town would be a better place if ...
   – This school would be a better place if ...

Show your sentences to your partner. Does he/she agree?

4 I wish I hadn't …

I wish + Past perfect • should(n't) have

<<< ARE YOU THE PERSON YOU'D LIKE TO BE? >>>

Analysing your regrets is the first step to finding out

From time to time, we all find ourselves regretting things we've done and things we haven't done. But there's no point in getting depressed about it. In fact, looking at our regrets can be a very useful way of finding out more about ourselves.

Try this test.

FIRST fill in the table. Put a tick against each regret, to show whether you feel it often, sometimes or never.

THEN add two more regrets that you often (or sometimes) feel.

Now look at the results. What do they tell you about yourself?

Here are ten common regrets. How often do you say them to yourself? Add two more of your own.	often	some-times	never
1 I shouldn't have lost my temper.			
2 I should have said what I really thought.			
3 I wish I'd kept my mouth shut.			
4 I wish I hadn't spent so much money.			
5 I shouldn't have left it to the last minute.			
6 I wish I'd been a bit friendlier.			
7 I should have offered to help.			
8 I wish I'd remembered …			
9 I shouldn't have let it upset me.			
10 I should have refused.			
11			
12			

1 Look at the sentences in the table.
   How do we use *I wish* and *I should* to express regret?

2 Read the article and follow the instructions.
   What do your answers tell you about yourself?

Grammar Checklist

would have done

would have + *past participle – to refer to the unreal past.*

I **would have** phoned you, but I was too busy. (= actually I didn't phone you)
I **wouldn't have** enjoyed living in the 16th century.

3rd conditional structures

If + *Past perfect* … **would have** + *past participle*

I **would have** phoned you if I **hadn't been** so busy.
If he'd **taken** a map, he **wouldn't have got** lost.
If **I'd known** they were at home, I **would have** visited them.
If she **hadn't left** the window open, the cat **wouldn't have got** in.

'Mixed' conditionals

These mix 2nd and 3rd conditionals. One part of the sentence is about the past, the other is about the present.

If he **hadn't stolen** the money, he **wouldn't be** in prison. (= he stole the money, so now he's in prison)
Inflation **would be** higher (now) if the Democrats **had won** the election (last year).

(For 2nd conditionals, see Unit 9.)

Structures for expressing regret

I wish + *Past perfect*

I wish **I'd apologised.**
I wish I **hadn't lost** my temper.

I should(n't) have + *Past participle*

I **should have** apologised.
I **shouldn't have lost** my temper.

See also Reference section, page 141.

Focus on Form

1 Would(n't) have done

For many years, Detective Shadow has been pursuing Sid Moriarty, a master of disguise and the cleverest criminal in North America ...

Read the story. How many reasons can *you* find?

Example:

Moriarty wouldn't have used his own sword. He would have used another weapon.

2 Past conditionals

Student A: **Read out the items from Box A. Use** *If + had(n't).*

Student B: **Complete each sentence with a suitable item from Box B. Use** *would(n't) have.*

Example:

A If they'd promised to lower taxes ...
B ... they would have won the election.

A	They didn't promise to lower taxes. They didn't know you were coming. They didn't have life-jackets. They lit a fire. They weren't insured. They didn't check the plane properly. The dog barked.

B	They were rescued. They drowned. They woke up. They didn't find the bomb. They ate all the food. They didn't win the election. They didn't get their money back.

3 Mixed conditionals

Put the verbs in brackets into the right form. Use the Past or Past perfect tense.

Example: *She wouldn't be so lonely* ...
... if she *knew* more people.
... if she *hadn't moved* away from home.

a They'd be much better off ...
   ... if they (not buy) such a big house.
   ... if they both (have) jobs.
b She'd still be at university ...
   ... if she (pass) her exams.
   ... if she (work) harder.
c He'd be much happier ...
   ... if he (live) in a warmer climate.
   ... if his wife (not leave) him.
   ... if he (not spend) all his savings.

Now make some continuations of your own.

'We've got him this time, sir!' the Sergeant told Shadow excitedly. 'It was Moriarty all right!'

'Tell me about it, Sergeant,' said Shadow.

'Well, sir, for a start, the victim was killed with a 17th century Italian sword, of a kind that Moriarty is known to have in his collection.'

'How do you know?' asked Shadow.

'We found it, sir. He dropped it in the hallway. And it's got his fingerprints on the handle. Not only that, a ring with *SM* engraved on it was found by the body.'

'Mm,' said Shadow. 'Anything else?'

'Plenty! It seems the victim didn't die immediately: he had time to write *MORIA* in his own blood before he died. And we found a note in his pocket: it said *Tonight you die*, and it was signed *Sid M.*'

'Is that all?' asked Shadow, smiling.

'Not quite,' said the Sergeant. 'There's a neighbour, a Mr Sam Crook, who says he saw someone answering Moriarty's description enter the building just before midnight.'

'Right,' replied Shadow. 'You'd better arrest Sam Crook.'

'Sam Crook, sir? But ...'

'Sergeant,' said Shadow patiently, 'I can think of at least seven reasons why Sid Moriarty didn't commit this crime.'

4 Regrets

Make sentences with *I wish* **or** *I should(n't)* **for these situations.**

Example: *You were behind a lorry on a narrow road; you tried to overtake it; you didn't see a car coming the other way, and you crashed.*

I shouldn't have overtaken the lorry.
I wish I'd seen the car coming the other way.
I should have been more careful.
I wish I hadn't crashed.

a You left school at 16; you didn't go to university; now you haven't got enough qualifications to get a good job.
b You found a briefcase lying on the pavement; you picked it up and opened it; it exploded, and now you're in hospital.
c You met someone you liked; he/she wanted to marry you but you weren't sure; he/she married someone else and now you're alone.

5 Pronunciation

How do you say the words and phrases below?

a I would have waited.
   You wouldn't have liked the film.
   If I'd known you were busy, I would have waited.

b If he hadn't left fingerprints, they wouldn't have caught him.

c I should have apologised.
   I shouldn't have bought it.

🔲 **Now listen and check your answers.**

24 Life on Earth

1 Global issues

1 Every week, a staggering 10,000 square kilometres of tropical rainforest are cut down. An area the size of France disappears every 12 months.

2 The nations of the world, rich and poor alike, continue to regard the sea as a convenient place to dump millions of tons of chemicals, sewage and industrial waste.

3 There are now more than 800 nuclear power stations throughout the world. Although this is supposed to be a 'clean' form of energy, there are in fact very high risks associated with it.

4 Smoke from factories and coal-fired power stations not only pollutes the air, but also causes chemical changes in the atmosphere which result in acid rain.

5 In 1985 it was noticed that there was a hole in the ozone layer over the Antarctic. Scientists now believe that the loss of ozone may be as much as 30%, and still rising.

6 Over the last 10 years, the Sahara has advanced southwards by an average of 20 kilometres per year, and 250,000 square kilometres of land has turned into desert.

7 A major report on global warming has warned that average world temperatures will rise by several degrees in the next century, due to the build-up of carbon dioxide and other 'greenhouse gases' in the Earth's atmosphere.

1 Look at the texts, and give a title to each one.
Which picture best illustrates each text? What's the connection?

2 Together, choose one of the issues. Then work in pairs.

Pair A: You think Pair B should be more worried about this issue. What will you say to them?

Pair B: You think Pair A are worrying about nothing. What will you say to them?

Now get together. Can you persuade the others to change their minds?

2 Going green

FIVE THINGS YOU CAN DO TO HELP THE ENVIRONMENT

❶ If it isn't very far, walk or cycle – leave the car at home.

❷ Have a shower instead of a bath.

❸ When you go shopping, don't ask for a bag – take one with you.

❹ Don't throw away old bottles – take them to a bottle bank.

❺ Don't buy furniture made from tropical hardwoods.

FIVE THINGS GOVERNMENTS COULD DO TO HELP THE ENVIRONMENT

❶ Double the price of petrol.

❷ Introduce water meters.

❸ Put a tax on plastic bags.

❹ Put a deposit on bottles to encourage people to return them.

❺ Ban the import of tropical hardwoods.

1 Which suggestions do you think are better – those for individuals or those for governments?

2 Add another pair of suggestions, one for individuals and one for governments. Ask other students which suggestion they think is better.

3 Endangered species

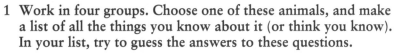

1 Work in four groups. Choose one of these animals, and make a list of all the things you know about it (or think you know). In your list, try to guess the answers to these questions.

– Where does it live?
– Why is it in danger?
– Roughly how many are there in the world?
– Is the number increasing or decreasing?

Turn to the back of the book and read about the animal. Were your guesses correct?

2 Tell other groups what you know about your animal.

Now hold a collection. Each student has $500 to spend on the animal(s) of their choice.

Which group collected the most money?

Death of the Dinosaurs

65 MILLION YEARS AGO, dinosaurs suddenly became extinct, together with a large number of other species. But why did it happen?

Many scientists believe that the cause was a large asteroid crashing into the Earth. According to this theory, the asteroid threw huge amounts of dust and water vapour into the atmosphere, blocking out the light of the sun, the vegetation died off, and the dinosaurs starved to death.

Evidence for the theory came in 1992 when scientists in Mexico uncovered an underground crater 175 kilometres wide, which turned out to be exactly 65 million years old. The crater was probably caused by an asteroid 10 km in diameter hitting the Earth at thousands of miles an hour, with the force of 70 million one-megaton bombs.

According to David Raup of the University of Chicago, this was just one of many such cases. He says that asteroids have caused more than half of species extinctions since life on Earth began 600 million years ago. If he's right, it seems likely that *Homo sapiens* will end its days in the same way.

READING

Find answers to these questions in the texts.

1 Look at the pictures at the top of page 109. Which shows
   – an asteroid?
   – a comet?

2 How did dinosaurs become extinct? What evidence is there?

3 Which asteroid has caused the most damage during the 20th century?

4 What damage would the following cause?
   – an asteroid 30 metres wide
   – an asteroid 1 kilometre wide
   – Swift-Tuttle's comet

5 What are the chances of
   – a 1 km wide asteroid hitting Earth during your lifetime?
   – a 5 km wide asteroid hitting Earth next year?
   – Swift-Tuttle's comet hitting Earth on August 14, 2116?

6 How is NASA planning to use
   – telescopes?
   – nuclear bombs?

DISCUSSION

1 Do you think that the human race will go the same way as the dinosaurs?

2 Do you think NASA's plans are
   – sensible?
   – pointless?
   – dangerous?

LISTENING

1 Imagine that you read the following headline in your daily newspaper:

10 KM ASTEROID HEADING FOR EARTH
**Due to arrive in 6 months' time
The chances of impact are 70%**

What would you do?

2 You will hear five people saying what they would do in the same situation.

If you had to spend the next six months with one of the speakers, which one would you choose?

ASTEROIDS AND COMETS

Asteroids are lumps of rock flying around in space. They are fragments of planets that have broken up.

Comets are chunks of ice surrounded by dust. The dust is visible as a long tail trailing behind the comet.

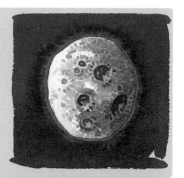

Some recent encounters with asteroids

1908
A 60-metre asteroid exploded in the air about 8 kilometres above the Tunguska region of Siberia, destroying hundreds of square kilometres of forest. The explosion was equivalent to 20 hydrogen bombs.

1978
A huge explosion equivalent to 100,000 tons of TNT was detected in the South Pacific. This was first thought to be a secret nuclear test, but most experts now think it was an asteroid strike.

1991
An asteroid 10 metres in diameter passed between the Earth and the Moon, scoring a near miss.

1992
An asteroid called Toutatis, measuring 3 km across, passed within 3 million km of Earth. Toutatis is a regular visitor, and in 2004 it is expected to come even closer, within 1.5 million km of Earth.

Size	How often?	Damage
10 m–100 m	every 300 years	Most explode on hitting the Earth's atmosphere, and cause no damage. Some of the larger ones, however, get through, including two this century. If either of these had arrived over a major city, millions of people would have been killed.
1 km	every 300,000 years	An asteroid this size could affect whole countries, with tens of millions of deaths in a densely populated region. The impact would throw up enough debris into the atmosphere to block out the light of the sun for several years.
5 km	every million years	This would be big enough to cause mass extinction. Agriculture and civilisation would certainly be destroyed, and the human race might not survive.

The bigger they are, the harder they fall: some vital statistics about asteroids

NASA to the rescue

As we can't predict when a really big asteroid will arrive, is there really any point in worrying about it? NASA thinks there is. It estimates that there are between 1,000 and 4,000 asteroids at least 1 kilometre in diameter which regularly cross Earth's orbit. If such an asteroid hits the Earth once every 300,000 years, this gives the average person roughly a one in 4,000 chance of being around when it happens. A small risk, maybe, but much bigger than the risk of dying in an air crash, which is one in 20,000.

NASA aims to set up six new telescopes and spend the next 25 years working out which large asteroids are likely to arrive within the next century or two.

The idea is that once they've identified an asteroid heading straight for us, they can move it out of the way by hitting it with powerful nuclear bombs. One expert recently proposed inventing a new nuclear bomb, 10,000 times as powerful as anything we have at the moment. He did not explain how.

August 14, 2116 – the End of the World?

Dateline 26 October 1992

WHILE SOME BELIEVE man-made pollution or a nuclear war may bring civilisation to a close, the end of the world is more likely to come in the shape of a huge chunk of ice and dust called Swift-Tuttle's comet, an Australian Conference was told yesterday.

New research indicates that its probable date of impact with Earth is August 14, 2116, said David Steel of the Anglo-Australian Observatory. It is not known if the collision will come in the morning or afternoon.

The size of Swift-Tuttle, which is travelling at 200,000 kph, is calculated at between five and 10 kilometres wide. The chance of collision is calculated at one in 400. Scientists

Adapted from *New Scientist, The Times.*

Review: Units 19–24

Find out

1 Find out what hobbies other students have got, and how long they've been doing them.

2 Find out about a time recently when your partner felt one of the following:

   – angry   – embarrassed   – nervous
   – frightened – worried   – jealous

3 Work in groups. Find out how 'green' other students are. How do they try to help the environment? What do they do that's bad for the environment? Who's the 'greenest' person in the group?

4 In groups, choose a TV programme that you all watched recently. What did you think of it?

Role-play

1 Choose one of these situations, and improvise a conversation:
   – A is interviewing B for a job.
   – A is a police officer who has just stopped B for driving too fast.
   – A is going through customs. B is a customs officer.

  Now report your conversation.

2 Imagine that you're a famous person (dead or alive). What is your main regret? See if other students can guess who you are.

3 A You're in favour of nuclear power.
  B You're against nuclear power.
  C You're a TV interviewer. Interview A and B for a TV documentary.

Conversational English

1 Making offers

That's very kind of you. My hands are rather dirty.

No, that's OK. I can hear it all right.

No thanks. I don't mind walking.

Yes, thanks. I'd love some.

Well, I'd love to, but I'm busy that evening.

Shall I …?
I'll … if you like.
Would you like me to …?

Do you want (to) …?
Would you like (to) …?

1 Here are some replies to offers. What offer do you think the other person made? Use expressions from the box.

   Now listen to the conversations.

2 Work in pairs.

Student A

B has got a lot of problems, and you want to help. Decide what you could do to help B with each problem.

Now get together with B. Keep making offers until you offer what B wants.

You've been thrown out of your flat.
You've hardly got any money.
If you find somewhere to live, you don't know how you can move all your things.
You haven't had a good meal for days.
The whole thing has made you ill and exhausted.

Student B

You've got a lot of problems, but A is going to help you. For each problem, decide exactly *how* you'd like A to help you.

Now get together with A. Keep refusing A's offers until he/she offers what you want.

Talking points

Choose one of these topics. Take it in turns to say a sentence or two about it.

It's ages since …

Getting old

Young people and the law

Things I can never remember

Showing your feelings

I'd be happier if …

Regrets

Are human beings an endangered species?

Words

1 Complete these questions:
   – What .... ice-cream do you want?
   – What .... shoes do you take?
   – What .... car do you drive?

2 Look at these remarks. What's happening?
   – 'There's no need to get so angry.'
   – 'Don't cry. It'll all turn out all right.'
   – 'No. I've already told you. I won't do it.'

3 Continue these lists:
   – wedding, bridgegroom …
   – funeral, coffin …
   – global warming, desertification …

2 In the street

1 Excuse me. Do you know …?

2 Excuse me. I wonder if you could tell me …?

3 Excuse me. Do you know …?

Yes. There's one just round the corner.

Yes. It's nearly half past three.

5 Excuse me. Could you tell me …?

Well there's a bank in the next street.

Yes. Carry on up here and it's the second on the left.

Excuse me. Can you tell me …?

4

I think it goes in about ten minutes.

1 *a* Complete the questions in these conversations.

   ▭ Now listen to the recording.

b Make these questions more polite.

   – Where's the station?
   – What time does the bank open?
   – Is there a bookshop near here?
   – Where can I buy a newspaper?

2 Think of a polite question to ask someone in the street outside your school. See how many people know the answer.

Additional material

1·Focus on Form·2 *Student A*

Text 1 **Ask B questions to find the missing words.**

The Tuareg live in .... People call them
..................., because they .... Both men and
women ...., as a protection against sand and
duststorms. Traditionally, the Tuareg breed ....,
and take .... across the Sahara. Nowadays, many
Tuareg live in ...., where they work as
....

Text 2 **Use this text to answer B's questions.**

The Dinka live in the southern
part of the Sudan. The men of the
tribe look after cattle, and they
regard them as extremely
important. When a boy grows up,
his father gives him a special bull,
and he looks after it for the rest of
its life. He plays with it and sings
songs to it, and when it dies he
mourns for it like a friend.
Although the Dinka get milk from
their cattle, they don't normally
eat them. If they want meat, they
usually hunt hippopotamus in the
River Nile.

3·Focus on Form·2 *Student A*

Use these facts to ask your partner questions.
The answers are the words in *italics*.

1 *Margaret Thatcher* became Prime Minister
   of Great Britain in 1979.
2 The Second World War began *in 1939*.
3 Archimedes was *having a bath* when he
   shouted 'Eureka'.
4 *Paul McCartney* wrote the song 'Yesterday'.
5 In the film 'From Russia with Love', *Sean
   Connery* played James Bond.

5·1 Overseas experience

Interplex

Qualifications
Applicants must be between 18 and 26 years old. They should
have a basic knowlege of English, and be physically fit. A driving
licence and experience in hotel work is an advantage but is not
essential.

Travel
Interplex International will pay 50% of the cost of return air or
train fare. This will be paid to employees on completion of their
contract.

Contracts and pay
Contracts will be for a minimum of 6 weeks. Employees will be
paid at standard local rates, and local tax and insurance will be
deducted.

Work permits will be arranged by Interplex International. Please
enclose *two* passport photos with your application form.

Conditions of work
Employees will do a variety of jobs, including cleaning,
bedmaking, acting as porters and waiters, helping in the kitchens,
and driving between the hotel and airports/stations.

The working day is from 6.00 am till 9.00 pm. This will include
two hours for meals, plus a two-hour free period which may be
from 10.00–12.00 or 2.30–4.30.

Employees will have one free day per week. This can be any day
except Saturday and Sunday.

Employees are expected to look smart at all times, and will be
provided with a uniform, which they must wear during working
hours. The hotel will be responsible for cleaning the uniforms.

Accommodation and food
Accommodation will be provided in the hotel or an annexe, in
rooms shared between four employees.

Meals will be provided free of charge by the hotel.

Hotel facilities
Outside working hours, employees may use the hotel's facilities,
including the swimming pool, sauna and tennis courts. They will
be charged for these at 40% of normal rates.

4·4 Can you make a million? *Cards 6–11*

6 You've had an astonishing two years. Not only did you get married, but your father-in-law died, leaving you a large house and an even larger sum of money. You invested it, and you now have £200,000 more than two years ago.

Your parents wrote to you recently, saying there's still a job open to you in the Civil Service if you want it. Or you could stay where you are, and carry on having beach barbecues.

Stay in Brazil	➤ **22** (p.116)
Join the Civil Service	➤ **16** (p.115)

7 You arrive in Los Angeles and manage to find a place to live, but there aren't many jobs around. After doing casual work for a time, you manage to get a job as a taxi driver – not a quick way to make a million dollars, but the money's not bad. At the end of two years, you've increased your total wealth by £10,000 – LA's an expensive place to live.

You could either stay in LA and drive your taxi, or go back home – there's still a job open for you in the Civil Service.

Stay in Los Angeles	➤ **25** (p.116)
Join the Civil Service	➤ **16** (p.115)

8 The country has been suffering from serious economic problems for more than a year now, and recently a lot of companies have gone bankrupt – including yours. You're unemployed, and there aren't any jobs in advertising – not even for someone as good as you. Still, you did well enough last year, and you now have £20,000 more than you had two years ago.

A friend told you about an interesting job you can get – working as a crew member on a yacht in the Caribbean, taking wealthy Americans to Caribbean islands. Otherwise, there's always the Civil Service ...

Go to the Caribbean	➤ **4** (p.23)
Join the Civil Service	➤ **16** (p.115)

9 For the last two years, you've been running your own business as a financial consultant. Unfortunately, running a business is more expensive than you imagined, and not enough people want your financial advice. At the end of two years, you have £5,000 less than you had when you resigned.

One day, your former boss rings you and asks you if you'd like your old job back. You accept the offer.

Rejoin the Civil Service	➤ **5** (p.23)

10 You had a good time at design college – it was very interesting and you made a lot of friends. Unfortunately, you also spent quite a lot of money: you now only have half of what you had two years ago.

You could now get a well-paid job in an established advertising agency. Alternatively, you could go to Brazil for a couple of years – a friend of yours is working there and says she could probably find you a job. You've heard the beaches are unbelievable ...

Go into advertising	➤ **19** (p.115)
Go to Brazil	➤ **14** (p.114)

11 You've joined the Civil Service, and you're finding the work quite interesting, although you aren't being promoted as fast as you hoped. Still, you're earning enough to buy your own flat and a car. In the last two years, you've become £20,000 better off.

You met a friend the other day who works in an advertising agency, and makes nearly twice as much money as you. It might be a good time to change jobs ...

Stay in the Civil Service	➤ **16** (p.115)
Go into advertising	➤ **19** (p.115)

7·2 Changes *Student A*

1·Focus on Form·2 *Student B*

Text 1 **Use this text to answer A's questions.**

The Tuareg live in the Sahara region of North Africa. People call them the 'Blue People', because they wear blue robes. Both men and women cover their faces with veils, as a protection against sand and duststorms. Traditionally, the Tuareg breed camels and take camel caravans across the Sahara. Nowadays, many Tuareg live in towns and cities, where they work as servants and nightwatchmen.

Text 2 **Ask A questions to find the missing words.**

The Dinka live in .... The men of the tribe look after ...., and they regard them as extremely important. When a boy grows up, his father gives him ...., and he looks after it for the rest of its life. He .... it and .... it, and when it dies he .... like a friend. Although the Dinka get .... from their cattle, they don't normally eat them. If they want meat, they usually hunt .... in the River Nile.

3·Focus on Form·2 *Student B*

Use these facts to ask your partner questions. The answers are the words in *italics*.

1 *Bill Clinton* beat George Bush in the 1992 American Presidential Election.
2 Isaac Newton was *sitting under an apple tree* when he discovered gravity.
3 *Napoleon* invaded Russia in 1812.
4 In Shakespeare's play, Othello killed *his wife Desdemona*.
5 Björn Borg won the men's tennis championship at Wimbledon *five times*.

4·4 Can you make a million? *Cards 12–15*

12 You're doing quite well at university, although economics isn't very interesting. If you carry on, you'll probably get a good degree. Or you could drop out and go on a two-year course at design college.

You're not spending much money – at the end of the two years you have £1,000 less than you had before.

Continue at university	➤ 2	(p.23)
Go to design college	➤ 10	(p.113)

13 So much for your career in the Civil Service! The government made huge cuts this year, and you were made redundant. Fortunately, you got a large redundancy payment – you now have £100,000 more than two years ago.

Now you have to look for a job – times are hard and you're not as young as you were. You could get a job with a firm of accountants. Or you could join a friend who's starting up a business designing children's toys. It's not a very good time for small businesses, but you never know ...

Join a firm of accountants	➤ 24	(p.116)
Go into the toy business	➤ 3	(p.23)

14 You've had a wonderful time in Brazil – beach barbecues, lots of parties, swimming ... Your friend helped you find a part-time job with a computer company – not very well paid, but it leaves you time to travel around and see Brazil. You've spent quite a lot of money on food and air fares, but you've still managed to save a bit. You have £5,000 more than two years ago.

Recently, you met someone you like a lot – you could settle down here. Alternatively, some friends of yours are travelling overland to the USA and have invited you to go with them.

Stay in Brazil	➤ 6	(p.113)
Go to the USA	➤ 20	(p.115)

15 The last two years have been bad for small businesses, including yours – you made a loss again in both years, and now have £25,000 less money than two years ago.

Designing toys is still hard work, and you and your friend are not working together quite as well as you were before. This might be the moment to give up and get that job with a firm of accountants. On the other hand, you've invested four years of your life in this business now ...

Stay in the toy business	➤ 21	(p.115)
Join a firm of accountants	➤ 24	(p.116)

4·4 Can you make a million? *Cards 16–21*

16 You're working in the Civil Service, and you're now £25,000 better off than you were two years ago. You're still in a fairly junior post, and your salary hasn't risen as much as you hoped. Never mind – it's a good steady job and you bought a new car this year.

On the other hand, several of your friends are self-employed, and this might be a good time to start your own business – as a financial adviser, for example …

Stay in the Civil Service	➤	**5**	(p.23)
Start your own business	➤	**9**	(p.113)

17 You've been round the world. You've seen temples in Bali, lions in Africa, penguins in the Antarctic, the Himalayas, the Grand Canyon … and you've spent and spent and spent.

After two years of luxurious travel, you now have only 25% of your money left, and it's time to go back home. The trouble is, you aren't so young any more, and there are two possibilities open to you. You could get a job with a firm of accountants. Or you could join a friend who's starting her own business designing children's toys …

Join a firm of accountants	➤	**24**	(p.116)
Go into the toy business	➤	**3**	(p.23)

18 In the last two years, you've increased your savings by £5,000. You've got a good steady job, but it isn't exactly exciting. If you carry on working here, you'll probably be a manager by the time you're 45 – but you certainly won't be a millionaire!

You'd do better to go back to university or design college and get some qualifications.

Go to university	➤	**12**	(p.114)
Go to design college	➤	**10**	(p.113)

19 This is the job for you. You've got a natural talent for it, and you really like the people you work for. Your company's designing a new series of soft drinks advertisements, so there's plenty of money coming in – at the end of the two years you have £45,000 more than you had before.

You're doing well, and there's no reason to change jobs at the moment – although your friend in Brazil wrote recently, inviting you to go there, and this could be your last chance …

Stay in advertising	➤	**8**	(p.113)
Go to Brazil	➤	**14**	(p.114)

20 Everything was fine until you got to a remote part of Central America, where you were kidnapped by bandits and held prisoner for two years. Eventually, you managed to buy your freedom, but it was expensive, and you're now down to your last £2,000.

One of your group has friends in Los Angeles – if you can get there you should be able to find a job. You've also heard that you can get jobs on yachts in the Caribbean, working as crew members for rich Americans – might be worth a try.

Go to the Caribbean	➤	**4**	(p.23)
Go to Los Angeles	➤	**7**	(p.113)

21 You're a genius! You designed a family of toy dinosaurs from outer space (called *Galactosaurs*) that became an instant success. They've sold all over the world, they appear on T-shirts, cups, bags, socks … There are even plans to make a series of cartoon films about them.

In the last two years, you have made a staggering £600,000.

You don't need to go anywhere from here: by now, you're either 36 years old or a millionaire – or both!

7·2 Changes *Student B*

7·1 Ancient civilisations

4·4 Can you make a million? *Cards 22–25*

22 Bad news! The Brazilian economy has collapsed and inflation is running at 30% a month. You can't find a job anywhere. Worse still, your partner has left you for someone else, and taken half the money. You now only have a third of what you had two years ago.

You've heard from a friend who's working on a yacht in the Caribbean as a member of the crew. He says he could get you a job too, and that the pay is quite good.

Or maybe it's time to go back home to the Civil Service ...

Go to the Caribbean	➤ 4	(p.23)
Join the Civil Service	➤ 16	(p.115)

23 You should have left the ship when you had the chance. On your last trip to Miami you were all arrested for smuggling gold and jewels (lucky for you it wasn't drugs or arms!). You were sentenced to six years in prison, and fined £10,000. Fortunately you've invested your money, which makes up for the fine.

Add *four* years to your life (you only served four years because of good behaviour): you have the same amount of money as before.

Someone you met in prison says he can help you get a job in Los Angeles. Or you could go back home and try the Civil Service (you'd better not tell them you've been in prison!).

Go to Los Angeles	➤ 7	(p.113)
Join the Civil Service	➤ 16	(p.115)

24 You're working for *Jarvis, Jarvis & Jarvis, Accountants, Ltd*. It's not the most interesting job in the world, but it's a safe, established firm, and the pay's reasonable.

Your friend in the toy business has found another partner, and there aren't any other good jobs around. It looks as if you'll be working here for at least another four years.

For each two-year period you work here, add 10% to your savings.

25 A year ago, you were driving your cab when you saw a couple fighting in the street. The woman shouted 'He's going to kill me!' and jumped into your cab. She turned out to be a Hollywood movie star – she gave you a large tip and asked for your address. Last month she died, leaving you £500,000 in her will, 'To the taxi driver who saved my life'. Add that to your savings, plus £10,000 from driving your taxi.

A friend back home is starting up a business designing children's toys and has invited you to join her – it might be a good way to invest all that money. Or you could celebrate by going on a trip round the world ...

Go into the toy business	➤ 3	(p.23)
Go round the world	➤ 17	(p.115)

A NEW ICE AGE?

MOST OF THE TALK these days is about global warming. But in fact the opposite could happen: it would only take the tiniest change in the Earth's orbit round the Sun to bring another Ice Age. A change of as little as 5°C would have a dramatic effect on life on Earth.

CLIMATE SHIFT

The main effect would be to shift climate about 1,500 kilometres towards the Equator, so that Spain, say, would have a climate much the same as England's is now, and Buenos Aires could look forward to the kind of weather now found around Cape Horn.

FOOD

The same would be true of crops: wheat would grow in Spain, but no longer in Britain; it would be impossible to grow rice in most of China; and grapes would be much happier growing in Africa than in France.

CATASTROPHE

In the colder regions of the world, the results would be devastating. Large parts of Northern Europe, Canada, Chile and Argentina would be covered in snow and quickly become uninhabitable. Huge numbers of people would be forced to migrate to warmer climates, bringing with them economic catastrophe, and probably war.

A sign of things to come?

TURNING THE DESERT GREEN

On the brighter side, a number of inhospitable places would become more pleasant to live in. Cave paintings in the Sahara Desert show that it was once full of people and animals. A drop in temperature – together with increased rainfall – might begin to turn the desert green again.

A cave painting in the Sahara, 1300 BC

12·2 Emergency

Snake bite
Movement helps the poison to spread, so try not to walk about: if possible, send someone else to get a doctor. Meanwhile, tie something (e.g. a handkerchief) fairly tightly above the bite, to stop the poison spreading. If you have a sharp knife, make a cut and suck out as much of the poison as you can.

Cut wrist
If possible get someone to call a doctor right away. Meanwhile, try to stop the bleeding: close the wound and apply pressure with your other hand (or get someone else to), until bleeding begins to stop. This may be some minutes. Any bandages should be applied tightly: if blood soaks through the bandage, don't remove it – just add another bandage on top.

Hotel fire
Wet towels or sheets and use them to block the gap under the door. Then open the window, try to attract the attention of people outside, and wait for help to arrive. If you can't open the window, and the room becomes smoky, go down to floor level: it's easier to breathe near the floor, because smoke rises upwards.

Boiling water
Reduce the heat as quickly as possible by putting the arm in cold water or under a cold tap for at least 10 minutes. Remove anything tight such as jewellery, and cover the burn with a clean smooth cloth to avoid infection. Then take the person to hospital.

Heart attack
If the patient is conscious, place her in a half-sitting position, with her head and shoulders supported with pillows or cushions, and with another cushion placed under her knees. Then call a doctor or an ambulance. Loosen clothing around the neck, chest and waist. Do *not* give the patient anything to eat or drink, and do *not* allow her to move unnecessarily.

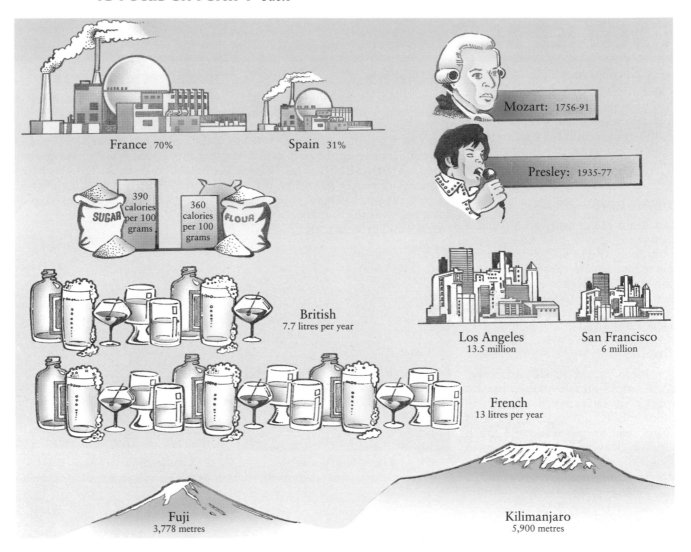

France 70%   Spain 31%

Mozart: 1756-91

Presley: 1935-77

390 calories per 100 grams (SUGAR)   360 calories per 100 grams (FLOUR)

British
7.7 litres per year

Los Angeles
13.5 million

San Francisco
6 million

French
13 litres per year

Fuji
3,778 metres

Kilimanjaro
5,900 metres

24·3 Endangered species: *pandas*

- Pandas are one of the rarest animals in the world. They live only in a small area in the mountains of South-western China.
- There are only 500–1,000 pandas surviving in the wild, and the number is decreasing all the time. There are about 100 more in zoos and research stations.
- Although they are protected, pandas are still poached for their skins. Because they are so rare, their skins are very valuable.
- Pandas live in mountain forests, and can only eat bamboo. As their habitat is getting smaller and smaller, pandas are in danger of dying from lack of suitable food.
- Zoos are making efforts to breed pandas in captivity, but this is very difficult. Also, baby pandas weigh only 100 grams at birth, so they need to be looked after very carefully. Since 1963 about 50 baby pandas have been born in captivity, and around half of them are still alive today.

15·Focus on Form·2 *Student A*

This is last week's news. Find out from B what has happened since then.

There were worries last night about the safety of the Claxton nuclear power station, after reports of leaks

The search is continuing in the French Alps for a party of schoolchildren who failed to return from a

There are rumours that the Louvre is planning to sell the priceless Mona Lisa, the most

A group of 200 refugees crossed the border last night without passports or visas and

Police were questioning billionaire Oliver James last night about the disappearance of millions of dollars

The Government has denied that Miss Botham is a spy, and has demanded that she should be released immediately and

Only 3,000 tickets have so far been sold for the 'Rock Show of the Century' due to take place

17·Focus on Form·3 *Student A*

My name's George.

I come from Texas.

I own an oil company.

I own three houses in the USA and one in the South of France.

I'm staying with the Foreign Minister.

I'm going to have dinner with the Prime Minister tomorrow.

I really like it here because there's so much to buy in the shops.

I've never been here before, but I'll certainly come again.

24·3 Endangered species: *tigers*

- There are six species of tiger still in existence. They are found in Siberia, India and South-east Asia.
- 50 years ago, tigers were common throughout much of Asia, living in many different habitats from tropical forest to semi-desert.
- Because people thought they were dangerous, they were hunted and trapped, and tiger skins were considered very valuable.
- By 1970, there were fewer than 5,000 tigers left, and many of their habitats had been destroyed.
- In 1972, Operation Tiger was launched: tigers were protected by law and reserves were created to protect the species.
- Gradually, numbers began to increase, and there are now some 8,000 tigers living in the wild.

17·Focus on Form·3 *Student B*

My name's Ramona.

I collect antiques.

I'm planning to open an antique shop here.

I often go to New York on business, and I always fly first class.

I've known the Rockefeller family for years.

I know lots of famous people in America.

It's lovely talking to you.

I'll give you a ring next week and we can have lunch together.

15·Focus on Form·2 *Student B*

This is today's news. Answer A's questions using the Present perfect tense, active or passive.

The power station will stay closed until engineers have

The schoolchildren were taken to Moutiers by helicopter after being found by rescue workers

The new owner of the Mona Lisa, billionaire Clara Fairbanks, who paid a record $900 million for

There were angry protests yesterday against the Government's decision to send back 200 refugees who had

Billionaire Oliver James was arrested last night on charges of fraud and theft. He will appear in court

Sarah Botham flew back home yesterday to be reunited with her family after her release from

Angry fans protested yesterday after the organisers cancelled the 'Rock Show of the Century', which

24·3 Endangered species: *rhinos*

- Most rhinos live in Africa. There are two African species: the black rhino, which lives in East Africa and the white rhino, which is found in Southern Africa. There are also a few rhinos in Asia, mainly in India.
- Over the last 20 years, numbers of rhinos have dropped rapidly: there are now fewer than 10,000 in the whole world, and the number is still falling.
- The main threat to rhinos is from poachers, who hunt them for their 'horns', which are in fact made of stiff hair. The horns are sold in the Middle East, where they are used to make dagger handles, and also in the Far East, where they are used in medicines and aphrodisiacs.
- Trading in rhino horn is illegal, but it is still continuing. Unless more is done to protect them, they will almost certainly become extinct.

15·2 Tell me more

23 Morrison Drive
Redbridge
Monday 16th

Dear Lucy and Fred,

Just to let you know that the baby's arrived! It's a girl, and we've called her Frances, after Theresa's mother. She's a lovely baby, with blue eyes and black hair.

We went into hospital at 9 o'clock last night, when the labour started, and the baby was born just after 2 o'clock this morning — not bad! Theresa was wonderful. I was there the whole time, and the birth wasn't too difficult this time, thank goodness, although she's a big baby — nearly 4 kilos!

Theresa is fine, and sends her love. They're coming out of hospital on Friday, so do come and see us next week some time.

Henry's seen his little sister, and seems quite excited by the whole thing. I expect he'll change his mind before long!

See you soon.

Love,
David

24·3 Endangered species: *elephants*

- Elephants are found in Africa and in Asia (mainly India). African elephants are slightly larger and have much bigger ears.
- Elephants in Africa are in serious danger: nearly a million have been killed in the last 10 years, and only about 600,000 are left.
- In Asia, there are only about 50,000 elephants left in the wild. However, Asian elephants are used for transporting timber, so many are now born in captivity.
- Elephants are killed by poachers for their tusks, which they sell as ivory. Elephant ivory is made into ornaments, piano keys, chopsticks and other objects.
- In 1989, governments of 79 countries agreed to ban all trade in ivory, and this ban came into effect in 1990. Unfortunately, as long as people buy ivory, poaching will continue and elephants will be in danger.

Tapescripts

1·4 At the moment …

1 I'm a journalist. I work for the *Daily Mirror*. I report on foreign news, so I spend quite a lot of time abroad. At the moment I'm covering the American elections.

2 I work as a secretary for a firm of accountants, so I answer the phone, type letters, things like that. At the moment I'm typing out our annual report, which I have to finish by Friday.

3 I'm a research student. I spend a lot of time in libraries and on the phone to people, trying to get information. I study the history of medicine, and at the moment I'm doing some research on the First World War, finding out what kind of medicines they used in the army.

4 I work on a farm, a potato farm. I drive a tractor and I help with all the jobs around the farm. There's not much going on at the moment, being winter. We're cutting down some of the trees and mending fences, mostly.

5 I work for the United Nations as an engineer. I'm involved in development projects in Africa. Just at the moment there's a big project we're doing – we're building a dam in Ethiopia.

2·1 Easy to live with?

1 Well, she helps a lot with cleaning the flat, but she's not very tidy. She always leaves books and magazines lying around, and she never puts things away when she's finished using them.

2 He's only been in a couple of weeks, but he's a good cook, and he's very tidy. He never makes a mess when he's cooking, and he always washes up afterwards.

3 Oh no, I like Jane – she's really great. Oh, apart from one thing – she spends hours in the bathroom. I can never get in to have a shower. And another thing – she uses up all the hot water.

4 Well, his room's always in rather a mess – he never tidies up, never puts his clothes away. Oh he's OK otherwise – he's quite quiet, doesn't make too much noise.

5 The worst thing about her is she leaves all the lights on. She never switches the light off when she goes out of the room, so I have to go round switching them off after her. And she leaves all the doors open.

2·3 A place to relax

A OK, I'd like you to imagine an ideal room, a place to relax.

B I see windows, big windows that look out on the sea. A small room with wooden walls, wooden furniture, wooden floors, a thick rug, a thick woollen rug on the floor, and a dog – I love dogs. On the floor also a table, a small table with papers, magazines, books on it. Music coming from a CD player.

A What about you? What are you doing?

B Reading. Listening to the music and reading at the same time. I'm reading a novel. And the room is warm – I'm alone.

2·4 Snow house

Now we'll cut a small hole for a chimney, and meanwhile John is packing snow over the outside just to make it all nice and strong and close up any gaps so the wind doesn't get through.

Now we're building the blocks round and round in a spiral. They're very firm, very firm, and there's no chance of them falling in.

Now we're cutting blocks from the floor of the igloo, so it will be below ground level, and we're building the walls from the inside.

So that's it, and it's very strong, you see – well, take a chance here, here we go. Yes, I can climb on the top of it, no problem, no problem. And it's very strong. So, it took just over an hour to build, and that's not bad for a place to live.

So now we've just got one block to put on the top. So I'm going to push it up through here and then let it fall into position – there, ah there, good. And now we're going to make the entrance tunnel.

Now I've marked out a circle for the igloo, and I'm cutting blocks from the entrance tunnel first. So this, this will go down below ground level.

Well, we've found some nice firm deep snow here, and it looks like a really good place to build an igloo. So we'll get started. So first of all we're going to mark out a shape for the tunnel and for the igloo itself.

3·3 The first time …

1 How did I learn to swim? It was when I was 11. It was just after we'd moved from Berlin to the south of Germany to a small village and I was the last one in the class of 28 who could not swim, but as I was very good in sports otherwise I decided that I will be able to swim in no time. So I didn't want to be taught, I just stepped on the diving board and jumped in and somehow struggled with the water and managed to move back to the side of the river bank and got out, and that was it.

2 I learnt to swim when I was about five or six during the summer holidays, and I remember my father putting me in the swimming pool in the shallow end and at the other end of the pool he put I think it was a chocolate bar on a plate, and he said 'If you can swim to the other end all on your own you can have the chocolate bar', and I did.

3 It was while I was at infants school, which would make me five or six, I suppose. My brother and I used to be taken for lessons on a Tuesday evening. My brother learnt to swim a lot sooner than I did, and so I used to watch him jumping into the deep end, while I was sort of guided up and down the shallow end on the end of a pole. I used to look forward to the hot chocolate that we used to buy in the foyer afterwards.

4·2 Exchanges

1 A Do you think you could lend me £20?
  B Um, well I'm not sure.
  A I can pay you back on Friday.
  B Well OK, here you are. (Thanks)

2 A I'd like to pay my bill, please.
  B Right, yes, it's all made out. There you are.
  A Thanks. Do you take credit cards?
  B No, I'm afraid we don't. You can pay by cheque or by cash if you've got it.

3 A I bought a shirt here the other day and it's got a little tear here (Oh yes, yes) on the back of the collar, so I'd like a refund please.
  B Right. Did you bring your receipt with you?
  A No, I haven't got one.
  B Well I'm afraid without the receipt we can't really give you a refund.

4 A Excuse me, I'm sorry to bother you. Can you give me change for a £10 note? I need to make a phone call and I haven't got any change.
  B Sorry, I can only give you change if you buy something.
  A Oh really? OK well, can I just buy some chewing gum, please?

5 A I'd like to cash some traveller's cheques, please.
  B Certainly. Can I see your passport? (Yes) Right. Thank you. OK, you'll need to sign them just here please.

4·4 Can you make a million?

A So Gareth, you're going to tell us how to make a million.

B Well, to go back to the beginning, um I went to study graphic design after leaving school. And I was there for two years, and when I left college I decided to go off and see a bit of the world.

A Where did you go?

B Well a friend of mine got a job in Brazil, so I decided to go and have a look at Brazil. And I had a wonderful time. The social life was terrific, and I made a lot of wonderful friends. Some of these friends then decided to drive up to the USA. It seemed like a very good opportunity to see some more of the world, so I joined them. But we had a bit of a mishap in Central America. We were kidnapped by bandits, believe it or not, (Good Lord) and it was two years before I got away from them.

A What an extraordinary experience …

B … And eventually that was the way that we escaped from them, by paying our way out.

A So what happened then?

B Well, having got away from there I went to the States, as I planned to do two years before, to Los Angeles, without any money of course, and for four years I drove a cab in LA.

A Did you meet any of the stars? …

B … But when she died only a year later, she left me half a million pounds in her will.

A That is extraordinary. What a stroke of luck. So what did you do?

B Well, fortunately a friend wrote to me to say that she was starting up her own toy-making business. So I came home and I worked helping her design, and of course business was very slow to start with. But then I had a great stroke of luck. I found a design that was very popular – I designed the Galactosaurs (Of course) which are a family of toy dinosaurs, and they proved to be a great hit all over the world. And that was the beginning of my great good fortune, and I've just become a millionaire.

A And congratulations.

5·3 Punishments

1 The worst punishment I can remember was when I was at primary school, and I'd stayed in the school building at lunch time, because I felt it was too cold to go out. And for that they made me go down to the class below, and do all their lessons for a whole week. And I wasn't even allowed to see my own friends during the break times.

2 I remember I was about seven and I got punished because I held my prayer book too low in morning prayers. They made me stand up in front of the class and recite a prayer in front of everybody, and I was terribly embarrassed.

3 When I was about eight years old and I was at school, I remember we were having a Latin lesson, and the teacher asked me something, and I was extremely rude back to him. And to punish me, he made me write out 'I must not be cheeky' something like 500 times in Latin one Saturday afternoon.

6·3 Festival

The Dragon Boat Festival commemorates the death of a national hero, Chow Yen, who threw himself into the river and drowned himself in protest against a corrupt Government, and that happened about oh over 2,000 years ago in China. But the people saw the incident and they felt very sorry for him, and they collected a fleet of boats and beat the drums, made a lot of noise and raced the boat in the river trying to scare away the creatures in the river which were about to eat Chow Yen's body. And other people made up dumplings of rice, meat, beans, and they threw these dumplings into the river to feed the fish and other creatures in the river. That's how it started originally.

And nowadays people still make dumplings but they do not throw the dumplings into the river any more. They eat the dumplings, which is really very delicious. And they still hold boat races, anywhere in China, in Hong Kong and any parts of the world where there is a sizeable Chinese community, they still hold dragon boat races. The dragon boats are quite narrow and long and they have the head of a dragon in the front and the tail of a dragon at the back and they have about 22 people on each boat. They have a drum, a big drum at the end of the boat as well, so while the people are racing one person will be beating the drum and the people have to row together to the rhythm of the drum.

6·4 Culture shock

I was travelling in the Sudan by train and the journey I had to make was going to last about 48 hours and about an hour into the journey someone in my compartment, I think there were another seven people in the compartment, someone spread a large cloth on the floor and people began to bring out food. No-one had a knife, so people were breaking up the food and placing it on the cloth …

… I realised this was the thing to do so all I had was three or four tomatoes. So I broke up my tomatoes and put them on the cloth and then we all started to eat the food. And there was bread and beans and lamb and many different things and people were eating and I noticed that no-one was eating my tomatoes. So I encouraged them to eat and everyone smiled very politely but wouldn't actually take any. And slowly the food disappeared and disappeared and my tomatoes were left. So at the end of the meal there was nothing left except my tomatoes. And I felt slightly uneasy about this, I didn't know why …

… I thought probably it was because I was a foreigner and perhaps the Sudanese people didn't want to take a foreigner's food from them. So in fact I ate the tomatoes myself. It was only some time later that I realised that in fact the reason that people hadn't eaten my tomatoes was because I had broken up the tomatoes with both hands.

● On the phone

1 A Hello. 305 8442.
  B Hello. Is that Carol?
  A Speaking.
  B Hi. This is Bill.

2 A Hello. Fletcher's Bookshop.
  B Hello. Could I speak to Mr Taylor, please?
  A Certainly. Can I have your name, please?
  B My name's Linda Holden.
  A Hold on. I'll put you through.

3 A Hello. Fletcher's Bookshop.
  B Hello. Could I speak to Mr Taylor, please?
  A I'm afraid he's not in at the moment.
  B Oh, OK. Can I leave a message?

7·4 For and against

1 Well I have to get up very early in the mornings, so I have to go to bed very early the night before. So it's great for me because I can, when there's good programmes on, I can record them late at night and watch them later on.

2 The problem is they just taste so awful. In the old days food used to really taste of something, but this stuff just tastes of nothing.

3 In the old days, say fifty years ago, nobody knew what was going on in the world. But nowadays you can actually see what's happening anywhere in the world, almost as it's happening.

4 I type with two fingers, and when I used to type letters I'd always make a mistake and then have to type the whole letter all over again – drove me crazy. But now I can just correct it on the screen as I go along, and when I'm happy with it I'm finished. It's perfect, brilliant.

5 At school I learnt how to add up in my head, and children just can't do that any more. My son can't add up at all.

8·2 What's the system?

1 To use a public telephone, first you lift the receiver and then you put in the coins. You can use as many coins as you like, because at the end of the call the coins which haven't been used are returned. And then after putting in the coins, you dial the number. Alternatively you can use a phone card, with which you can talk until the number of units on the telephone card has been used up.

2 To use libraries in England, you join the library. They'll give you a ticket, that means that you can keep books that you take out for up to two weeks. If you bring the books back late you have to pay a fine. There's also a reference section which you can use, but you can't take those books out, you can just use the books in the library.

3 To send a parcel abroad, you take the parcel to the post office, and have it weighed. And they give you stamps, which you stick on the parcel, and they also give you a customs form which you have to fill in, and then you stick that on the parcel as well. Now if you want to send something valuable, then it's normal to send that by registered post, which is rather more expensive than normal post.

8·4 Jobs we love to hate

1 I hate it when you ring up a big company, for example, and you're trying to get through to someone, and all you get is the ▮▮▮▮▮▮ who tells you to hold the line. And then they just leave you there – they don't tell you what they're doing, sometimes they play a horrible little tune that repeats itself over and over again, and you just – you don't know what's happening at all. And it's particularly annoying if it's a long-distance call, because it's costing a lot of money.

2 I don't like ▮▮▮▮▮▮ because I think that a lot of the time they take advantage of your vote. And they tell you that they're going to do one thing, but they're not, they don't have any intention of doing it. They're liars, basically. And I think that you put your trust in them by giving them your vote, and nine out of ten times they let you down.

3 I hate ▮▮▮▮▮▮, you know the people who ring you up and try and sell you something over the phone. And they always start off with a really stupid question like 'Would you like to make more money?' or 'Do you care about the environment?' And they always seem to ring up at the worst possible moment, like when you've just sat down to have tea or something. And they sound so cheerful, they really annoy me.

4 Oh, ▮▮▮▮▮▮ that try and sell you things that you don't want. You go into a shop, you want to buy a dress, you try it on, it doesn't look good, you come back out of the changing room and say 'No, thank you'. The ▮▮▮▮▮▮ says 'Oh well why don't you try another size?' You say 'No, I'm fine about it, I don't want it.' 'Oh well why don't you try another colour?' 'No, I don't want another colour.' They won't let you get out of the shop – it drives me mad.

9·1 What would you do?

A Your teenage daughter has started using the telephone to chat to her friends in the evening and quite often she talks for more than an hour, and it means that you can't use the phone yourself. Now you've told her to stop phoning her friends but now her friends phone her instead. Now what would you do about that? Rebecca?

B Oh it's a difficult one. I think I'd try to reason with her and say – I mean I wouldn't say 'You must not ring your friends and your friends must not ring you' because I think that's unfair. What I would say is 'If your friends ring you, can you just keep the conversation a bit short so that other people can use the phone?', which seems quite reasonable to me.

A Nick, what do you think?

C I think what I'd do is stop my daughter from answering the phone and monitor the calls as they came in. And she would only be allowed to take one call in the evening from a friend, and any other calls that came in from her friends, we'd say 'No I'm sorry, she's already talked to Angela or Julia or whatever and so she can't talk to anyone else' and take control of it that way.

A Aisha, do you agree with that?

D Not really. I think you should always try and remember what it felt like at that age and actually how important it felt to try and talk to your friends. What I'd do I think is really encourage her to visit her friends and to have her friends round more so they could actually talk in person rather than on the telephone.

9·4 Wishes

– I wish I could take more time off work. I work at home, and I find it very difficult to stop at the end of the day.

– I wish I had time to do more exercise. I used to do a lot of aerobics, but now that I'm studying I find that I have very little time to attend the classes.

– I wish I could play the guitar. I used to try to teach myself, but I wasn't very good, so I gave up.

– I really wish it was warmer in the North of England, that's where I study, and I pay a lot of money for the rent and electricity to heat up the house. It would make me a lot happier to study in a warmer country.

– I wish I didn't have such an old car. I'd like to have one with central door locking and power steering and an open sun roof.

– I wish I lived in a smaller house. The house that I live in at the moment is very big. There are six of us living there, and it gets very noisy sometimes. In a smaller house I'd feel more comfortable and I'd have the quiet that I need to study.

– I wish my children would leave home. They're over 20, but they're still living with us, and they use the telephone all the time, and they invite all their friends around, and they're very nice kids but I just wish they'd go.

10·1 I don't know what it's called but …

1 I need a pair of those things you use for pulling nails out. They look like scissors but they're not sharp.

2 Have you got one of those spoons that I can use because I'm frying eggs in the frying pan and I need something to turn them over. You know those big spoons made of metal I can use.

3 Please, I'm writing my composition and I've made a mistake. Do you have this white stuff that you use for correcting mistakes? You know, it's got a little brush and you paint it over the wrong word.

4 Have you got one of those things to eat Chinese food? You know those long sticks, and they're usually made of wood or plastic.

5 I'd just like to find out how much fatter I've become. Have you got this thing I can stand on and find out how much I weigh?

10·4 Great ideas?

1 It looks rather dangerous because if you were at the top of a hill could you hold yourself so that you just didn't go down the hill really, really fast? I don't know. And then it says here that it floats on the water. Well that's fine, but if you were in a fast moving river and you were trying to get across, surely the water would take you with it and you'd just go on and on and never be seen again.

2 This is called a natural flying machine, but it doesn't seem very natural to me. How do you get the man inside, in the middle bit of this machine? And where do you find ten eagles? How do you actually put them inside their jackets? And just because we know that eagles can carry heavy weights, I mean we don't know how long they can carry heavy weights for. So they

may be able to lift a man for ten seconds or something, but they may not be able to keep going. But it's a nice idea.

3 My main fear is that it looks really claustrophobic once you're in there, especially with the lid down. It says you can have enough supply of food, a month's supply of food and drinking water in there – I'm a bit worried about the smell, for instance, of the food going off. Also, there's no mention of how you go to the toilet in it. Also, I should imagine you'd get quite seasick in it, especially with the lid on.

11·3 In five years' time

A So when are you planning to leave for Australia?

B I'll be going in a few months' time. I'm supposed to be staying there at least five years, but I don't know, I'll have to wait and see if I like it.

A And do you have a job to go to?

B Oh yes, I'm a nurse. I'm going mainly for the job that I've found there. I've found quite a good job in a university hospital, and I get a free apartment and I'll be earning twice as much as I do now, so it's not bad.

A That's good. And are you going by yourself?

B No, no I'm going with my boyfriend, who will by then be my husband. We're getting married before we go.

A And is he going to be working out there?

B Well hopefully he'll find a teaching job out there.

A And will you stay in one place in Australia?

B Oh I hope not. We really want to travel as much as possible. There's so much to see, I mean the whole of the Far East and the Pacific Islands, yeah.

A So you won't be starting a family straight away?

B Er, not just yet.

12·1 Narrow escapes

1 Well I had these friends round to dinner and, I don't know, for some reason I had this candle and I put it on the plastic lid of the record player, and forgot all about it. We went into another room to have some coffee, and I went into the kitchen to get some more coffee for a top-up, and as I went out I noticed this dreadful smell of burning. And I realised that the lid of the record player was on fire, and I looked in, there was this thick black smoke everywhere. So, well I didn't really know what to do – so I thought 'Don't throw water, get a wet towel', and I threw that over the record player lid, and went to call the fire brigade. And luckily everything was OK.

2 Well my mother tells me that when I was small, just around about a year, I very nearly drowned. I was playing by the pond in the garden, and apparently I slipped and fell in, and somehow I stood up just enough so my mouth was sticking out above the water. And I didn't cry out – I was apparently just too busy trying to breathe. And eventually my mother, who was wondering where I'd got to, came out, found me standing in the pond with my head just above the water, and she pulled me out before anything bad happened.

3 Oh, it was awful. I'd left some money on the table, and I turned round just for a second to do the dinner, and the baby put it in his mouth. It got stuck in his throat, and he couldn't breathe properly – he was choking. Well I had no idea what to do, so I called an ambulance ... But what happened was Jacky, my next-door neighbour was there, and she just turned the baby upside down, slapped him on the back, and the coin came out.

12·4 You're on your own

A Forward on the controls. That's fine. Let the aeroplane fly itself.

B I wish it would.

A Read the air speed.

B The air speed is about 105.

A I am on your right-hand side. Just relax ...

A ... We are going to do a left-hand circuit. Try to keep that height. Keep the turn going all the way round again.

B I understand but how do you stop it?

A Maintain the height, little more power. That's good. Keep turning to the left. Roll the aircraft in a gentle bank to the left. That's fine. Gently bank to the left, if necessary a little bit of power ...

A ... I'm going to attempt to get you down.

B Going down, are we?

A We are shortly, yes. Bank gently to the right. We are aiming for the wide tarmac strip to the right of the white and red lights. Can you see it?

B Affirmative.

A Pull back very gently on the control column. Close the throttle, just hold it there. Hold it. Hold it. Hold it. Hold the control column back. Relax. OK ...

A ... Press the top of the rudder pedals. You will find the brakes. Press both rudder pedals together ... you will find the brakes.

B The engine still hasn't stopped.

A Can you see some keys in the ignition?

B Affirmative.

A Turn the keys to 'off' and take them out. The engine should then stop.

B The key's out.

A Has the engine stopped?

B Just stopping now.

A Unstrap yourself and the emergency services will see to you.

B Thank God.

A You're welcome. All in a day's work.

Making suggestions

– Shall we drive down to the coast?
– We could always just have some bread and cheese.
– Let's have an early night.
– I suppose we could just talk to each other.
– What about going for a picnic?
– Let's go and get a Coke.
– We could always play cards.
– Why don't we try that new restaurant?
– Why don't you go and sit in the shade?
– How about getting a take-away pizza?

13·1 National differences

1 In France most of the people want to have a very long time for lunch. In Britain it doesn't seem to be important because people take a cup of tea and a very quick sandwich and it's OK.

2 Another very surprising thing for the foreigner is the way the people obey the law – you seem to have much more discipline than in France, and you respect the police much more than we do. For instance, people park their car everywhere, and they know it is forbidden but they do it – in Britain people don't do that.

3 In England it's easier to feel alone, people don't bother you, don't look after you or worry about you so much, so it's easy to get sort of, to get lost or to hide away here. When you're in the United States people want to know who you are, they tend to speak to you, to find out who you are, what you're doing.

4 Yes, one thing I should mention is that the United States is I think a much more exciting place to be than England, but there is a drawback and that is, you do have this sense of danger in the United States, especially in big cities, that you don't get so much in England or Britain as a whole. You feel safe in England.

5 Japanese houses are really small and people live close to each other, and there aren't so many parks, there aren't so many places where you can play when you are little, and it's very difficult for people to relax.

6 Japan is quite safe, and you can leave your handbag behind when you leave the room without being really careful about it. But in Britain you really have to keep eye on your handbag when you leave the room, and you have to take it with you when you leave.

14·2 Changing channels

And our next guest has come all the way from the United States to be with us tonight. Ladies and gentlemen, Michael Douglas!

It is not yet clear exactly how the accident happened, but police believe that the lorry driver swerved to avoid a child. The driver is …

(Sound of cars and guns)

It's amazing to think that I am standing at the very spot where, two and a half thousand years ago, the Athenian and Persian armies met at the battle of Marathon. Since then, of course, …

And as they come into the last lap, it's still the Kenyan way out in front, and if he can keep this up he could be on his way to a new world record. And …

Aw, you wouldn't want to shoot a friendly little rabbit now, would you? …

– Samantha – your question for £200. What is a *didgeridoo*?
– A kind of bird?
– Come in. Oh. It's you. What do you want?
– I just … wanted to say I was sorry about yesterday.
– A bit late for that, isn't it?

Hello? Anyone here? Hello?

14·4 Easy listening

1 Sometimes in the mornings I use it as an alarm clock. It's got three different timers and the first alarm that goes off usually starts off with the seashore and seagulls and I listen to that for about 15 minutes. And the next one comes on which is, wakes me up a bit more is more like south-east Asian pop music. And then I get the World Service news at 8 o'clock in the morning to finally wake me up.

2 Also there are these *karaoke* channels, about maybe four or five of them I think. And *karaoke* is the thing where you sing along to background music and you have a microphone and you can become a pop star for a few minutes and sing along to the music so I use this a lot now. I've learnt a few of the Japanese songs now. I can sing maybe five or six of them.

3 About the alibi channels, I did actually use one once. I'd been out quite late one night and overslept and was late for work. So I just got hold of the radio, flipped onto the alibi channel, which is the sound of, sounds as though you're in a phone box in the street with passing cars and sort of horns going. And I turned it up fairly loud, put my telephone next to it and explained to the secretary at work that I was on my way to the office and I'd been to a meeting which started at 8.30 in the morning.

4 Also there are various kinds of music, you can get Indian music and Mexican music for example. So when I'm at home cooking and cooking a Mexican meal and I get my friends to come over and we put the Mexican channel on so it creates a nice atmosphere for dinner.

15·1 In the news

The news at 6 o'clock.

The body of American TV presenter Clive Robbins has been found off the coast of Florida. Mr Robbins was reported missing two days ago when he failed to appear for breakfast on his yacht while on holiday in the Florida Keys. The body was found shortly after 6 o'clock this morning by a rescue helicopter, and was flown immediately to Miami for a post-mortem examination.

Two people have been killed in an explosion which badly damaged a house in South-east London early this afternoon. First reports say that the explosion was caused by a bomb, and a number of bombs and other weapons have been found in the house. Police believe that a group of terrorists were using the house as a weapons store, and that the bomb went off accidentally.

And finally, thieves got a nasty surprise when they stole a van from a motorway service station yesterday afternoon. When they finally opened the van, which belongs to the Kent Wildlife Park, they found two tigers inside, which were on their way to the Wildlife Park from London Zoo. The thieves, obviously animal lovers, immediately phoned the Wildlife Park, who have now recovered their van – and the tigers – unharmed.

15·4 Eavesdropping

Part 1

A I don't think you can blame me just because you've been sleeping badly. It's hardly my fault, is it?
B I didn't blame you, I didn't, I never blamed you, I just said I'm, I think I'll go to bed early because I've not, you know, I didn't sleep very well.
A Yeah OK but you seem to imply that just because I'm not working that somehow I'm just you know sitting around doing nothing.
B I just said I was going to bed early because I was very tired. I slept very badly last night, I'm tired, I've got a busy, you know, busy day ahead of me.
A Oh, oh and I haven't. (Well) Because I'm just going to be sitting around watching television and twiddling my thumbs.
B I didn't say that, did I? Look I'm sorry you haven't got enough to do. I'm sorry that you're bored.

A I've got plenty to do, thank you very much. I've been out looking for five different jobs.

Part 2

1 A We've just got to do something. I mean she came home again after midnight last night.
  B I know, she hasn't looked at a book for weeks. She's never going to pass her exams at this rate.
2 A I bet you'll be glad to see them go, won't you?
  B Yeah, it's exhausting, I mean it's nice to see them because they live so far away, but, well it is hard work.
3 A He's so different. He used to be so shy and quiet.
  B I know, it really is incredible. I think he's changed since his divorce, don't you?

16·1 In the classroom

1 We sat in the dark and we watched these slides of different paintings and monuments and it was quite enjoyable.
2 We learnt a lot of dates and we learnt a lot about battles and kings and queens but we never learnt anything about ordinary people who had lived ordinary lives.
3 We did a lot of singing but if you wanted to learn to play an instrument you had to pass a special test.
4 I think my teachers mostly focused on grammar, but we also had the chance to speak in, during the class.
5 I remember we had a map of the world and we used to spin it around and wherever we put our finger on we used to study the country wherever our finger had landed.
6 We had the chance to do a lot of our own experiments which was very good because it gave you the opportunity to see how things worked.
7 We had a very good teacher and we used to write a lot of stories and a lot of poems and I really enjoyed writing poetry. That was great.

16·3 Going through the system

A At what age do children start school in the States?
B Generally six. That's when I started.
A And that goes up to what age?
B That goes up to grade six, so that would be what? Twelve years old? And then you go to seventh grade in Junior High School, in fact you go for three years to a Junior High School, 7th, 8th and 9th grades.
A And then you go to real High School?
B And then comes the real thing, three years of High School. That's the 10th, the 11th and 12th grades.
A And that takes you up to what age? Sixteen or …?
B Seventeen, eighteen. It's quite

common to finish High School with your Diploma at age seventeen.

A And how many subjects do you take for your Diploma?

B Well that depends on what type of Diploma you're doing. There are really two types – there's an academic Diploma, which would prepare you for College, and there's a non-academic Diploma, which is more vocationally orientated. Both types of Diploma have their compulsory subjects, you know, like in the academic Diploma you have to do English. But then in both cases again the student has some choice, so in addition there are what's called 'electives'.

A 'Electives' means you can choose the subject …?

B Exactly, exactly. So in the United States you could do a credit in driving, for example, and learn to drive at High School. Or typing is another skill that you can learn in High School, and that will count towards your Diploma.

16·4 Improve your memory

A OK I gather you've got an interesting way of learning words in a foreign language.

B Yes it's actually a very easy way of learning foreign words. What you do is to, you think of a word in your own language, in my case English, which sounds something like the word you're trying to learn and then you just imagine a picture in your mind which links the two ideas – the idea of the foreign word and the idea of the English word.

A Can you give me an example?

B Yeah, an easy example is the Greek word *skylos* which means 'dog'. And this immediately reminds me of the English words *ski* and *loss*, so I just imagine a picture of a skier on a mountain, one of his skis has come off and he's lost it and there's a dog carrying it back to him in his mouth. An example from a different language might be the Japanese word for 'thank you' which is *arigato*. Now that sounds to me a little bit like *alligator*, so I could imagine a rather unpleasant picture of somebody whose leg has just been eaten by an alligator and the alligator's smiling and saying 'Thank you very much.'

A OK I'm going to try you out with some words in Russian (Goodness. Russian, yeah) You don't know Russian, do you?

B No no no.

A OK. Well here's the Russian word for 'teacher', which is *uchitelj*.

B Could you say it again?

A *Uchitelj.*

B *U-chit-elj.* Oh that's easy. The middle

of this word is the English word *cheat*, which is something we often associate with teachers and students. So I can imagine a student sitting in an examination and he's cheating, he's copying from the student sitting next to him. And the teacher is standing over him saying 'You cheat!'

A OK, here's another word. It's the Russian word for 'fire' which is *ogonj*. *Ogonj.*

B *Ogonj.* Mm. Oh yes, again, let's take the middle of the word, *gone*. We think of a fire perhaps that's gone out. So I just imagine a picture of a fire in a fireplace and it's gone out. Easy.

A OK. Thank you. I'll try it as a technique.

17·4 The dead rabbit

Well, this friend of mine had a dog, which he'd bought for his daughter's tenth birthday. This dog was always getting into trouble, and it had already completely wrecked their house and dug up their garden.

Anyway, one Friday this dog turned up with a dead rabbit in its mouth, which it brought into the house and dropped on the floor. And my friend's daughter immediately recognised this rabbit as the one that belonged to the little boy next door, and the little boy kept this rabbit in a hutch in his garden, so the dog must have got into their garden and killed it.

So my friend had a look at the rabbit, which was all muddy and dirty, but it didn't seem to have any tooth marks on it and it wasn't damaged in any way. So he had an idea.

What he did was he cleaned the rabbit up and he dried it with a hairdryer, and made it look really nice, and then later on that night when the neighbours had gone to sleep, he slipped over the garden fence and put the dead rabbit back in its hutch. The next morning there was a ring at the doorbell, and it was the little boy's mother, and she was looking really upset. And my friend said 'What's the matter?'

And she said 'It's terrible. It's little Timmy's rabbit. I just can't understand it. The rabbit died two days ago, and so we took it out of its hutch and buried it in the garden, and this morning he went back out into the garden to clean out the rabbit hutch so we could sell it – and there was the rabbit back in the hutch.'

18·3 Guilty or not guilty?

And now the swordstick trial. Mr Edward Cook has been found guilty of carrying an offensive weapon. He was given a 28-day suspended prison sentence, and fined £200. He was also ordered to pay £2,500 towards the costs of the trial, and to hand over his swordstick to the police. Afterwards, Mr

Cook said he was shocked at the verdict, and repeated that he had only used the swordstick in self-defence. 'I had to use it,' he told reporters, 'or I'd be a dead man today.'

18·4 Detective Shadow

A *(Reading)* There was a loud crack of thunder and the power went off. Shadow started to look for a candle when he heard a knock at his door. It was Harry Fox, who lived nearby with his uncle. 'Come quickly!' cried Harry Fox. 'My Uncle Cecil has been shot!' Shadow grabbed a torch and ran to his neighbour's house. When they arrived, Shadow shone the light on Cecil's face, and he knew immediately that he was dead. Harry explained that he and his uncle had been watching TV, when suddenly the window had smashed in and Cecil had fallen forward dead. 'At that moment there was a crash of thunder and the power went out,' Harry said. 'That's when I ran and got you.' Just then the power returned and the two reading lights in the room came on. Shadow and Harry sat in total silence for two minutes, unable to believe the terrible scene before them. Shadow finally turned to Harry and said, 'Your story is obviously completely untrue.' Why does Shadow think Harry's lying?

B So right. So Shadow was in his house (Mm) and Harry Fox and his uncle were nearby, they're neighbours (Mm-hm) …

B … Erm, they sat in silence. So the television didn't come on then when the power came on.

A No.

B Ah, right. So in other words Harry had been lying. And that's how Shadow knew, because Harry had said they were watching the television. If they were watching the television, it would have come on again. So, is that right?

A Absolutely right, yes (Good). If Harry Fox and his Uncle Cecil were watching TV, as Harry claimed, the TV should have come back on when the power returned. They sat in silence for a couple of minutes, so it was obvious that the TV had not been on.

B Been on. Ah, OK, yeah.

A Well done.

Making choices

1 A What about this one? Is that the kind of thing you have in mind?

B Um, no, I'd prefer something a little darker.

A Mm. Well, there's this one.

B Yes, that's better. I'll have that one.

2 A Come on. Are you ready?

B Um, actually, I don't think I'll come, if you don't mind. I'd rather get on with this book.

3 A I'll have the chicken, please.
B One chicken … And for you sir?
A I'd like the lamb, please.

4 A Well we could drive. Or would you rather go by train?
B Well actually, I'd prefer to fly, if we can afford it.

19·3 It's a long time since …

1 When I was in France I used to go dancing every, every week, and I haven't been dancing since September, which is several months now. And I really miss it because I would go there every Monday, I remember. So I'm just quite looking forward to doing it again when I go back to France.

2 The last time I played football was when I used to live in South Africa, because it was quite warm and we used to play all year round, it was never cold or anything like that, so that was quite fun. That was about seven years ago that I really, really enjoyed playing football all the time. Then when I moved to England it was a lot colder, and we had to play football in the cold, in shorts, and it was freezing, so I didn't really enjoy it then and I gave it up quite soon after that.

3 It's two years since I last went ice-skating, and I used to really enjoy ice-skating because you could go with a big group of friends, and you could go for a long time, about three hours. But I haven't been for a very long time now because it's got more expensive and because I don't seem to have very much time.

20·1 Birth, marriage and death

1 After the burial it's very traditional to celebrate the death. And we celebrate that by eating and drinking and in some cases singing traditional Irish songs. Because we consider it to be a happy occasion, especially if the person is old, and they've, they're going to heaven and they're going to be rewarded in the afterlife.

2 The bride is dressed up and she sits in a chair surrounded by flowers and children, and everybody troops past to have a look at her. And then you just sit down, and you're given lots of sweets and drinks, soft drinks. And then the groom and his entourage arrive, and he takes her hand and leads her away.

3 In Scotland, there's a tradition related to birth, where you must present the baby with a piece of silver, a silver coin. And you have to take this coin and actually place it in the baby's hand and make the baby hold it. The idea behind this is that the baby will be rich in later life.

4 After the death of the person, this person's corpse will be taken to the furnace, where the corpse is cremated. And afterwards from the furnace bones are taken out. And all the family members get together to pick up the bones with chopsticks. Each relative takes one bone and put them in a small jar, and we bury it.

5 The bride is dressed in white and the bridegroom is dressed in a black suit and white shirt. At midnight she goes away and takes off her white dress and puts on a red dress. She comes back to dance with the guests, and the guests pay for dancing with her, so she dances with everybody and when she's ready and when the bridegroom thinks that's enough, then he takes her by the hand and they run away and they take all the money with them.

20·4 A Good Boy, Griffith

Section 5
The next afternoon he went up the hill to the red brick cottage again. He saw the lace curtains move suddenly as he approached, and the door opened before he had even time to reach the knocker.

'Come back?' she asked. 'If you've not got the money you might as well turn around and go.'

'Steady, steady, girl,' said Griffith, 'don't get so jumpy. I've got the money. Have you got the ring?'

He took the roll of white notes from his waistcoat pocket. 'Come on in then,' she said.

With a quick turn she walked from the room and he heard her going up the stairs. Then she came slowly down.

'There's your ring,' she said, half throwing it on the table. 'Keep it. I'd rather have the money.'

Griffith took the ring. 'One more thing,' he said. 'Nobody must know.'

'All right,' she said quietly. 'Morgan didn't even know I had the thing. I told him I'd given it back to you.'

Section 6
When Morgan came home he washed the grease from his hands under the tap then sat down to his meal. Blodwen poured the tea unsteadily.

'What's up, Blod?' he said. 'You don't look so good, girl.'

'I'm all right,' she said.

'Was Griffith here today?' he said casually, cutting a thick slice from the loaf.

She went pale but he did not look up. 'Yes,' she admitted.

He laughed. 'Good boy, Griff, you know. Sort of steady chap. Can't see why you didn't marry him. Always trust him.'

'Does it matter now?'

'No,' he replied good-humouredly. 'The thing is, did he bring the fifty quid?'

Blodwen felt her heart capsize. 'Yes,' she said shakily. 'Yes, he did …'

Her husband nodded. 'Good boy, Griff. Came in and asked me to lend it to him so he could get a real special ring for his girl Gwen. Nice girl. Said he'd get it from his savings when his dad came home from the pit and bring it up here. A good boy, Griff; yes a good boy …'

21·3 Getting to know you

1 A Hi. Which class are you in?
B I'm studying Japanese.
A Oh, I'm in the same class. (Ah) Yeah, I've just joined, this is my first time. Are you enjoying it?
B Yes, I am. It's fine.
A Have you ever been to Japan?
B I've been once, yes.

2 A Hi. I'm Ian. Do you know anyone here?
B Only a few people. Oh, I'm Alison. (Hi) Do you know anyone here?
A Er just Bob, who I, I think it's his party actually, he met me when he came in.
B Yes. Are you from the States?
A No, I'm from Canada, but you know, it's sort of the same accent, but I'm Canadian, actually.

3 A Excuse me, how long have you been waiting?
B Um, about half an hour now. These buses are always late.
A Are you going to town?
B Yes, yes I am.
A Are you going shopping?
B Er no, I'm meeting a friend there.

21·4 Tags

1 It's a bit cold today, isn't it?
2 They speak Arabic in Iran, don't they?
3 You haven't seen my glasses, have you?
4 Auckland isn't the capital of New Zealand, is it?
5 They didn't stay very long, did they?
6 That film was awful, wasn't it?
7 Penguins can't fly, can they?

22·2 Reactions

1 A Happy birthday, Annie.
B Oh thank you! Can I open it now?
A Of course.
B Oh it's lovely. Thank you very much.

2 A What's the matter?
B My girlfriend Mary just walked right by me in the street and didn't even say hello.
A Maybe she didn't see you.
B She saw me all right. She's just, I don't know, mad at me or something.
A I'm sure she isn't darling – don't get too worried about it. She probably just didn't see you.

3 A Do you want to go for a walk?
B No I've got far too much work to do.
A Oh please, it's a lovely day.
B I know, but let's go later, eh?

4 A Would you mind keeping the noise down, please? I'm trying to get to sleep, I've got to get up early in the morning, this has been going on for two hours.
B Yeah well I'm sorry. It's just, a friend of mine's just got married, you see. We're having a party.
A Ah well I hope he's very happy. The thing is I've got to get up early. When are you going to stop?
5 A Is anything the matter?
B It's Caroline. She's left me.
A Oh no. I don't believe it. What happened?
B Oh nothing really happened. She just said she was moving out and she didn't want to see me any more. I think she's met someone else.
A Oh that's terrible. Look, tell you what, I'll make us some coffee, and then we'll get in the car and go for a drive.

22·4 What's in a smile

A So you've just been on a smile therapy course. What was it like?
B It was really good. I enjoyed it.
A What did you have to do on the course?
B We started off by doing breathing exercises so we could feel about breathing in happiness and of course we had to smile, we had to smile a lot, and the idea is that if you smile you feel better, it puts you in a good mood, so we tried that. We had to try to remember the last time we felt happy and think about that feeling. Then we were given a lecture and that helped to explain how we forget to laugh. When we grow up we forget to laugh. As children you play and you laugh and you smile and you have fun and as you get older life is much more serious. And they're trying to help us to go back to that feeling of childhood and the fun that we had.
A So did you do any activities on the course?
B Yes, they got us into groups, and we had to think back to things that had made us laugh. That was really interesting because it's surprising how there's some people who just can't remember what last made them laugh.
A What about you? Could you remember?
B Oh yes I could remember because I watch funny things on the telly.
A And what else happened on the course?
B Well, the last bit was really the best. That's when they put on a tape of somebody laughing and they were just laughing really out of control and it was really good because we all started to laugh and one by one everybody was laughing because laughing is infectious and that was really good fun.

A What about homework? Do you do anything at home in between the sessions?
B Oh yes, we have this homework to do. We have to practise to laugh. It sounds a bit strange at first, you have to stand in front of the mirror and laugh, sort of like laugh at yourself, which the first time feels embarrassing but it does work and it makes you feel better. Yes. It's good.
A So in general do you think the course has helped to make you feel better about yourself?
B Yeah I do and it is good fun, and it's nice to be with a group, and I can think of some bad-tempered people who I would recommend should go on it.

23·1 Dilemmas

1 Well this is very difficult, but I'm vegetarian, and I don't think I could have eaten the flesh of another person. I don't think I could have lived with myself afterwards if I'd survived. So no, I wouldn't have eaten the flesh of another human being.
2 I think I would have eaten the flesh of the other passengers. If I looked at it from a point of view that I was one of the dead passengers, I wouldn't have minded my body helping other people live. So I think I would have reluctantly done it.
3 I think I probably would have ended up eating the flesh of my fellow passengers if I needed to to survive. I find the idea physically revolting when I think about it, but I don't find it morally revolting. I don't see any moral reason for not doing that if it's necessary to survive, so I probably would have done.
4 I would not have eaten the flesh of my fellow passengers, quite simply because I believe it's morally wrong to do so. So if it was a choice between starving to death and eating the body of another person, I would have chosen starvation.

24·4 The Doomsday Asteroid

1 Well if I only had one month left to live I'd certainly live it up. I'd spend every penny I have, I'd run up an enormous overdraft at the bank, buy everything I've ever wanted, eat anything I've ever wanted to eat, I don't care how bad it is for me – I'd just have a wild time.
2 I think I would go to Spain and get a really nice house on the beach, and have a month on the beach with my children, playing by the seaside, just having fun.
3 I'd buy a wonderful pair of walking boots and an enormous rucksack, and set off with my partner to walk around the entire coast of the British

Isles and just stick to the coast, and just keep going, until the end.
4 Well it isn't absolutely certain that the world would end in six months, so I think I'd probably just carry on as normal really. But I think I'd try and do all those things that I've always wanted to do that I've never done. Like I'd learn to fly, and I'd try parachute-jumping, and I think I'd like to go scuba-diving. And that's what I'd do. I'd live normally, but I'd make sure that I really filled up my time with enjoyable things.
5 I suppose in such a situation, most people would just want to travel around. So I would open a travel agency and organise trips to the most exotic places, just like palm beaches, and exotic islands, visiting relations, and so on and so forth. And I would just earn a fantastic amount of money. There is a 30% chance that the asteroid wouldn't hit the Earth, so I'd become just fantastically rich. And when everybody goes to work after the panic has gone I would just retire and enjoy myself.

Making offers

1 A Would you like me to open the door for you?
B That's very kind of you. My hands are rather dirty.
2 A Shall I turn the volume up a bit?
B No, that's OK. I can hear it all right.
3 A I'll give you a lift to the station if you like.
B No thanks. I don't mind walking.
4 A Do you want some cream on it?
B Yes, thanks. I'd love some.
5 A Would you like to come to a concert on Friday?
B Well I'd love to, but I'm busy that evening.

In the street

1 A Excuse me. Do you know if there's a Post Office near here?
B Yes. There's one just round the corner.
2 A Excuse me. I wonder if you could tell me what the time is.
B Yes. It's nearly half past three.
3 A Excuse me. Do you know if there's anywhere around here I can change some money?
B Well there's a bank in the next street.
4 A Excuse me. Can you tell me when the bus leaves?
B I think it goes in about ten minutes.
5 A Excuse me. Could you tell me the way to North Street?
B Yes. Carry on up here and it's the second on the left.

Reference section

1 Regular events

Present simple tense

- We use the Present simple:
  - to talk about repeated or habitual actions:
    I often *go* to Berlin.
    He *has* a shower every morning.
  - for talking 'in general':
    I *enjoy* dancing.
    She *studies* music.
- To focus on *what happens* rather than *who does it*, we often use the *passive* form:
  The bridge *is painted* every five years.
  BMWs *are made* in Germany.
  In Britain, most babies *are born* in hospital.
- Active forms:

I	work don't work	at weekends.
She	works doesn't work	

Do you Does she	like horror movies?

- Passive forms:

Wheat is Potatoes are	grown in England.

Is wheat Are potatoes	grown in England?

Frequency expressions

once twice three times …	a day a week a year …	(once) every 6	hours days months years

- Often we can choose between two frequency expressions with the same meaning:
  every 6 months = twice a year.

Present continuous tense

- We use the Present continuous tense to talk about:
  - things happening 'now', at the moment of speaking:
    They*'re watching* the news.
    The Earth *is* gradually *warming* up.
  - current activities, things happening 'around now':
    I*'m going* out a lot at the moment.
    Everyone*'s wearing* hats this year.
- Compare the Present simple and continuous in talking about jobs and what they involve:
  I'm a history teacher. I *teach* class 2B. At the moment we*'re doing* a project on the Russian Revolution.

2 Around the house

Behaviour at home

- Some things you are supposed to do (and not to do) in your house or flat:
  - *tidy* things *up* and *put them away* when you've finished using them (don't *leave* them lying around)
  - *wash up* (or *wash the dishes*) after a meal, and *clear* things *away*
  - *keep* your room *clean* and tidy (don't *make a mess*)
  - don't *make* too much *noise*
  - *switch/turn* lights *off* when you leave a room (don't *leave* them *on*)
  - don't *use up* too much hot water.

Jobs in the home

- Labour-saving devices (= machines or appliances that save time and work in the home):

Appliance	Activity
vacuum cleaner	cleaning carpets
washing machine	washing clothes
sewing machine	sewing, making clothes
food processor	preparing food
cooker	cooking food
microwave oven	cooking food quickly
electric drill	repairing things, drilling
iron	ironing clothes
dishwasher	washing dishes

- Vacuum cleaners are also called *hoovers*, and we use the expression *to hoover the carpets*.
- *Cooker* is only used for the appliance. A person who cooks is a *cook*.
- *do the* + *-ing* is used for regular activities. It is only used if no noun follows (we say *do the cleaning* but not ~~*do the cleaning the floors*~~). Compare:

do the washing	wash the clothes
do the washing up	wash the dishes
do the cleaning	clean the floor
do the cooking	cook a meal
do the ironing	iron the clothes

Describing rooms

- Features of a living room:
  Rooms may have old or modern *furniture*.
  This may include *armchairs*, a *sofa*, or *bookshelves*.
  People often use *rugs*, *cushions* and *plants* to add colour to a room, and put *ornaments*, *pictures* or *photographs* round the walls.
  The walls may be *painted* or have *wallpaper*.
  The room may have doors or *French windows* (= glass doors) leading onto a *balcony* or a *patio*.

3 Past events

Past simple and continuous tenses

- We use the Past simple to talk about things that happened in the past:
  He *went* abroad in 1980.
  They *arrived* at 1 o'clock.
- Positive and negative forms:

I He	saw didn't see	the film.

- We use the Past continuous to talk about the background to past events (things that were going on at the time):
  The children *were playing* outside.
  I *was having* lunch (when they arrived).
- Positive and negative forms:

I was(n't) We were(n't)	feeling very tired.

- The Past simple and continuous are often joined with *when*, *while* or *as*:
  I was having lunch *when* someone rang the doorbell.
  A woman came up to me *while* I was walking home.
  They arrived just *as* I was leaving.

Past time expressions

- *when* can be followed by Past simple or continuous:
  I met her *when* I was on holiday.
  I met her *when* I was living in London.
- *during* is followed by a noun phrase:
  I met her *during* the summer holidays.
- *before* & *after* can be followed by Past simple or -*ing*:

Before I *went* Before *going*	to college, I worked as a waiter.

Subject and object questions

- Subject questions ask about the subject of the sentence. They keep normal word order:
  Someone *told* you → Who *told* you?
  Something *happened* → What *happened*?
- Object questions ask about other parts of the sentence. They have question word order:
  You *told* someone → Who *did* you *tell*?
  You *left* it somewhere → Where *did* you *leave* it?
  She *was eating* something → What *was* she *eating*?

Past simple passive

- We often use the Past simple passive to focus on *what happened* rather than what people did:
  He *was killed* in a road accident.
  The baby *was born* last night.
- Forms of the Past simple passive:

The building was(n't) The buildings were(n't)	damaged in the fire.

Was the building Were the buildings	damaged in the fire?

4 Money

Cost

- It *cost* £20.
  I *paid* £20 *for* it.
  I *bought* it *for* £20.
  I *spent* £200 *on* clothes.
- It's *cheap* = it doesn't cost much.
  It's *expensive* = it costs a lot.
  I can't *afford* (to buy) it. (= It's too expensive for me.)
- You should buy it – it's (*well*) *worth the money*.

Don't buy it – it's	*a waste of money.* *not worth the money.*

  These jeans are *good value* (*for money*). (= They're not expensive considering how good they are.)
  These jeans are a *bargain*. (= They're cheaper than they should be.)

Using money

At a bank	open/close an account, pay in / draw out money, cash a cheque
At an exchange office	change money, cash traveller's cheques, change francs into dollars
In a shop	buy something, ask the price, pay for it, get a receipt, bring it back, get a refund
In a hotel, restaurant, etc.	pay the bill, pay by cheque / by credit card / in cash

- Useful expressions:
  How much is it? How much does it cost?
  Do you take credit cards?
  Will you accept a cheque?
  Can you give me change for £10?
  Have you got any change?
- *lend* = give money (for a time).
  borrow = take money (for a time).
  Can you *lend* me $50?
  Could I *borrow* $50 (from you)?
  I'll *pay* you *back* next week.

The cost of living

Bills	medical bills, heating (fuel) bills, repair bills, rent
Taxes	income tax, sales tax, car tax, VAT (= European Community tax)
Insurance	property insurance, health insurance, life insurance, car insurance

- Some things that governments do:
  – *introduce* or *abolish* taxes
  – *increase* or *reduce* taxes
  – *spend money on* health, transport, education, defence, housing.

5 Obligation

Obligation and permission

have to need to (must)	don't have to don't need to (needn't)
can are allowed to	can't aren't allowed to (mustn't)

- *don't have to* and *don't need to* mean 'it isn't necessary':
  You *don't have to* bring any food with you (it's provided).
- *can* and *can't* are modal verbs. They are followed by the infinitive without 'to':
  We *can't* go in that room.
- *must*, *mustn't* and *needn't* are mainly used for giving orders or instructions. Compare:
  Parent to teenager: You *must* be home by 11; you *mustn't* stay out later than that.
  Teenager to friend: I *have to* be home by 11; I'm *not allowed to* stay out later than that.

make and let

- They *make* me stay in = I have to stay in.
  They *don't make* me stay in = I don't have to stay in.
  They *let me* go out = I'm allowed to go out.
  They *don't let* me go out = I'm not allowed to go out.
- Like modals, *make* and *let* are followed by infinitive without 'to', but they have the form of normal verbs:
  She *lets* her children *stay* up late.
  They *didn't make* us *wear* a uniform.
- Past tense forms:

I had to stay in. They made me stay in.	I didn't have to stay in. They didn't make me stay in.
I was allowed to go out. They let me go out.	I wasn't allowed to go out. They didn't let me go out.

Freedom from obligation

- Two ways of expressing freedom from obligation: structures with *-ever* and structures with *any-*:

You can do it	wherever *or* anywhere whenever *or* any time however *or* any way	you like.
You can see	whatever *or* anything whoever *or* anyone	

- With adjectives and adverbs, we use *as ... as ...*:

You can sing as	loud often much many songs	as you like.

6 On holiday

Holidays

- We say *go on holiday* and *be on holiday*:
  They're on holiday in Italy.
- The period when children are not at school is called *the holidays* (e.g. the summer holidays) or *the vacation* (e.g. the summer vacation).
- A day when people don't work (e.g. May 1st, New Year's Day) is a *national holiday* or *public holiday*.
- *Festivals* are special occasions (e.g. Christmas, Ramadan, Carnival) which people *celebrate* by taking part in *traditional* activities.

Types of holiday

- A holiday that is organised and paid for in advance is called a *package holiday*:
  They went on a package holiday to Ibiza.
- Some common types of holiday:
  – a seaside holiday (at a seaside resort)
  – a walking holiday
  – a camping holiday (at a camp site)
  – a coach tour (going from place to place by coach)
  – a cruise (going from place to place by ship)
  – an activity holiday (doing a special activity, e.g. painting, climbing, sailing).

Holiday activities

beach	sunbathing, swimming, waterskiing, windsurfing, diving
mountains and lakes	walking, climbing, skiing, camping sailing, canoeing, fishing
towns and cities	sightseeing, visiting churches, cathedrals, mosques, museums, art galleries, castles

- for activities we use *go + -ing*, e.g. go skiing, go camping, go fishing.
- You *go on* a journey, a trip, a tour, a picnic, an excursion (= a short organised trip).
- Cathedrals, castles, etc., are *sights* (= things people go to see). Tourists often *go sightseeing* or *see the sights*.
- Things that come from the place we visit are *local*. So we talk about *local specialities* (in restaurants) and *local produce* (in shops and markets).

Some things to take on holiday

clothes	anorak, T-shirts, swimming costume, shorts, walking boots, trainers, sandals
equipment	tent, sleeping bag, skis, face mask, map, camera, film, binoculars, beach mat
first aid kit	insect repellent, aspirin, suntan cream
luggage	suitcase, bag, rucksack (or backpack)
documents	passport, traveller's cheques, tickets, (international) driver's licence, insurance

7 Past and present

used to

- We use *used to* to talk about:
  - repeated actions in the past:
    I *used to* get up at six every morning.
  - past states:
    I *used to* live in the country.
- *Used to* emphasises that these actions or states are no longer true:
  I *used to* get up at six (but now I get up later).
  I *used to* live in the country (but now I live in town).
- Instead of *used to*, we can use the Past simple tense:
  I *got up* at six when I was at school.
- Forms of *used to*:

I	used to didn't use to	play with dolls.
Did you use to play with dolls?		

Note: We can also say *used not to*, but this sounds more formal.

- *Used to* is only used in the past, and has no present form. Note the difference between:
  - I *used to* ride a bike. (= I rode a bike earlier, but I don't now.)
  - I'*m used to riding* a bike. (= I often do it, I'm accustomed to it.)

Present perfect tense

- We use the Present perfect tense to talk about recent events:
  I'*ve finished* the book.
  They'*ve arrived*.
  (See also Unit 15.)
- We often use this tense to talk about *changes* that have taken place (what is different now from before):
  BEFORE: He used to be single.
  NOW: He's married.
  CHANGE: He'*s got* married.
- Active forms:

I've (= have) He's (= has)	mended the window.
Have you mended the window?	

- Passive forms:

The windows have The window has	been mended.
Have the windows Has the window	been mended?

- Some common verbs of change:
  get: The weather has got worse.
  become: Jazz has become less popular.
  start: I've started wearing glasses.
  stop: I've stopped seeing her.

8 At your service

Services

Place	You can …
dentist's	have your teeth filled/cleaned
garage	have your car repaired/serviced
electrician's	have your TV mended/repaired
hairdresser's	have your hair cut/washed
optician's	have your eyes tested
dry cleaner's	have your clothes cleaned
photographer's	have your photograph taken

- Instead of *have your hair cut*, we can also say *have a haircut*.
- Shops and places that offer services often add -'*s*, e.g. we can say *baker* or *baker's* (= *baker's shop*), *hairdresser* or *hairdresser's*, *optician* or *optician's*. Nowadays, the apostrophe is often left out.

Having things done

- If other people do things for us, we say that we *have* these things *done*, e.g. We have our windows cleaned once a month. (= Someone cleans them for us.)
- *Have something done* is a form of the passive. Compare:
  Someone *cleans* our windows once a month.
  Our windows *are cleaned* once a month.
  We *have* our windows *cleaned* once a month.
- Like the passive, the structure *have something done* can be used in any tense – past, present or future:
  I *had* my car serviced yesterday.
  I usually *have* my car serviced at Johnson's Garage.
  I think I'*ll have* my car serviced soon.

Systems

- *Using a public library*
  If you want to *borrow* books from a library, you have to *join* or *become a member*. To borrow a book, you show your *ticket* to the *librarian*, and *return* it (or *bring it back*) after a week or two. Most libraries also have a *reference section*, where you can read *reference books* (e.g. dictionaries, encyclopaedias, atlases).
- *Using a public phone*
  To make a *call* from a public *phone box*, you *pick up the receiver* and put in some money. You *dial the number*, and wait till the person answers. If the number is *engaged*, you'll have to try again later.
- *Sending things by post*
  You can *post a letter* in a *post box*, but if you want to send a *parcel*, you have to take it to the *post office*. There they will *weigh* it, and sell you *stamps* to put on it. You can send letters and parcels abroad *by air mail* or *by surface mail*. You can send valuable things *by registered post*.

9 Imagining

Conditional structures

1st conditional

> If + Present tense, ... will/won't ...

- We use the first conditional to talk about things that we think might happen in the future:
  If I *find* your watch, I'*ll* tell you.
  (You've lost your watch, and I'll look for it – perhaps I'll find it.)
- In first conditionals, we use *if* + Present tense to talk about the future.

2nd conditional

> If + Past tense, ... would/wouldn't ...

- We use the second conditional to *imagine* things that we don't expect to happen:
  If I *found* a watch in the street, I'*d* take it to the police.
  (No-one has really lost a watch – I'm just imagining the situation.)
- We also use the second conditional to imagine things that can't be true:
  If I *lived* in Hawaii, I'*d* go swimming every morning.
  (I don't live in Hawaii – I'm just imagining it.)
- To form second conditionals, the verbs move 'one tense back' from the first conditional:
    Present   →   Past
    will   →   would
  Note: in second conditionals the Past tense does *not* refer to *past time* – it is used to show that the condition is *unreal*.
- In second conditionals, we can use *were* instead of *was*. This is used in a more formal style, and also in the phrase *If I were you*:
  If he *were* older, I'd take him swimming.
  If I *were* you, I'd see a doctor.
- To talk about imaginary situations, we can also use *would* on its own:
  I don't think I'*d* enjoy having children. They'*d* take up too much of my time, and I *wouldn't* be able to go out and enjoy myself.

I wish

I wish	I *had* more money. I *could* go home. he'*d* stop shouting.

- After *I wish*, we use Past tense or *could/would*.
- We use *I wish* + Past to talk about the present:
  I wish I *had* a car.
  (I don't have a car.)
- We use *I wish* + *could/would* to talk about things we want to do and things we want to happen:
  I wish I *could* go out.
  (I want to go out but I can't.)
  I wish they'*d* pay me more money.
  (I want them to pay me more but they won't.)

10 Describing things

Ways of describing objects

shape	round, square, oval, triangular; flat
dimensions	long, short; wide, narrow; thick, thin
texture	rough, smooth; hard, soft
material	made of wood, metal, plastic, rubber, glass, pottery

- Expressions with adjectives: a glass bottle, a plastic cup, a metal table, a wood*en* spoon.
- *made of* = the actual material:
  The bottle is *made of* glass.
  made from = the original material:
  Glass is *made from* sand.

Use

- *use for*:
  You *use* a corkscrew *for opening* bottles.
  A corkscrew *is used for opening* bottles.
- Noun phrases:

-ing + noun	noun + noun	noun + -er/-or
writing paper frying pan washing powder	table lamp face cream kitchen knife	can opener pencil sharpener word processor

  – writing paper = paper you use for writing
  – table lamp = a lamp you put on the table
  – can opener = something you use for opening cans.
- Some commonly used nouns are written as one word:
  penknife, newspaper, notebook, saucepan.
- General words for describing objects:
  It's a *thing* you use for opening bottles.
  It's a kind of white *liquid* which is used for correcting typing mistakes.
  It's soft, coloured *stuff* that children use for making models.

Features

- My car *has got* electric windows.
  I've got a car *with* electric windows.
- His guitar *has got* 12 strings.
  He's got a *12-string* guitar.

Buying and selling

- To save money, you can buy things *second-hand* (= someone else has owned them before you). To find second-hand things, you can look through the *classified advertisements* (or *small ads*) in newspapers, which tell you what people have *for sale*.
- Some questions you might ask:
  – How much does it cost?
  – How long have you had it?
  – Is it in good condition?
  – Does it work?

11 The future

will, won't and might

- *will*, *won't* and *might* are followed by the infinitive (without *to*):

He	will (probably) might (probably) won't	give up his job. go and live abroad. become a novelist.

might = perhaps he will.
probably comes after *will* but before *won't*.

- *will*, *might* and *won't* can also be followed by the passive infinitive (*be* + past participle):

He	will (probably) might (probably) won't	be invited to the party. be released from prison. be promoted.

expect and hope

I expect I don't expect	the President will resign.

I hope	the President resigns. the President doesn't resign.

- *I hope* is usually followed by the Present simple, but it is also possible to use the future:
I hope the President *will/won't* resign.
- *I hope* is not used in the negative form (we can't say 'I don't hope …').

Future continuous and Future perfect tenses

- We use the Future continuous tense to say what will be *going on* at a point in the future.

In 5 years' time I'll	be living in London. be working for Esso.

- We use the Future perfect tense to say what will be *completed* at a point in the future:

By next month he'll	have left university. have found a job.

Linking expressions

- *in case* and *so that* are followed by the Present simple tense to express the future.
- *Otherwise* usually begins a new sentence.

You should take a torch	*because* it might get dark. *in case* it gets dark.
	so that you can see. *Otherwise* you won't be able to see.

12 Accidents

Accidents and injuries

- If you *have an accident*, you may *injure* yourself. If the *injury* is serious, you may have to go to hospital for *treatment*.
- Common accidents and injuries:
  - Oil splashed out of the pan and he *burnt* his hand.
  - The knife slipped and she *cut* herself.
  - He tripped and *twisted* his ankle.
  - She fell and *broke* her leg.
  - He touched the wire and *got an electric shock*.
  - She was going upstairs when she *had a heart attack*.
  - The roof collapsed and they *were trapped*.
- Expressions connected with fire:
  - The candle fell over and *set fire to* the carpet.
  - The carpet *caught fire*.
  - The carpet was *on fire*.
  - They tried to *put the fire out*.

Accidental death verbs

Verb	Cause
suffocate	you can't breathe
choke	something sticks in your throat
drown	your face is under water
starve	you have nothing to eat
die of thirst	you have nothing to drink

- There are many expressions with the form *die of* + noun: die of exhaustion, die of cold, die of old age.

Acting in an emergency

- In an emergency, you may need to *call for help*, *call an ambulance* or *the fire brigade*, or *give first aid*.
- Other common actions:
  - Keep the person calm/warm/still.
  - Comfort the person, stay with him/her.
  - If he/she has a cut, clean it, put a plaster on it or a bandage round it.

Driving

- To go faster, you *accelerate* (or *speed up*).
To go slower, you *slow down*.
To stop, you *brake* (or *put the brake on*).
If a car is going slowly in front of you, you can *overtake* it.
- To avoid something on the road, you may need to *swerve*.
If the road is wet or icy, you may *skid*.
If you aren't careful, you may *crash into* another car, or you may *run* someone *over*.

13 Comparing and evaluating

Comparison of adjectives

- My car isn't nearly as fast = his car is much faster. (a big difference)
  My car isn't quite as fast = his car is slightly faster. (a small difference)

His car is	much far a bit slightly	faster more expensive	than mine.

My car isn't	nearly quite	as	fast expensive	as his.

- We can also make positive sentences with … *as* … *as*:
  I'm (just) *as* clever *as* you.
  She's nearly *as* tall *as* her mother.

Comparison of adverbs

- If the adverb is formed by adding *-ly*, add *more*: quickly – more quickly; easily – more easily.
- If the adverb is the same as the adjective, add *-er*: hard – harder; fast – faster; early – earlier.
- Irregular: well – better.

too and enough

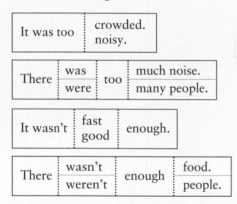

It was too	crowded. noisy.

There	was were	too	much noise. many people.

It wasn't	fast good	enough.

There	wasn't weren't	enough	food. people.

- *too* is followed by an adjective or adverb, or by *much/many* + noun.
- *enough* comes after adjectives and adverbs, but before nouns.

too/enough + infinitive

He was too ill. He couldn't go to work.
→ He was *too* ill to go to work.
The table was too heavy. I couldn't lift it.
→ The table was *too* heavy (for me) *to* lift.
  (*not* … to lift it)
The water wasn't warm enough. We couldn't swim in it.
→ The water wasn't warm *enough* (for us) *to* swim in.
  (*not* … to swim in it)

14 The media

- *The media* is a general term describing newspapers and magazines ('the Press') and radio and television. It is also called the *mass media*, because it brings information to large numbers of people.

Newspapers and magazines

- You buy newspapers and magazines from a *newsagent* or *news-stand* (or, in some countries, from a *kiosk*).
- Most newspapers appear *daily* or *weekly* (*once a week*). Magazines are usually produced *weekly*, *fortnightly* (*once a fortnight*) or *monthly* (*once a month*).
- Newspapers contain *articles* and *features*, which are written by *journalists*. Usually they also have a *leading article* or *editorial*, which is written by the *editor* and gives the point of view of the newspaper.
- In many countries, the press is *independent*, and newspapers may be *right-wing* or *left-wing*. In some countries, the press is *controlled* by the state and may be *censored*.
- Typical contents of a newspaper:

news	home news, foreign/international news, business/financial news, sports news
regular features	weather forecast, TV & radio programmes, horoscope, cartoons, letters, reviews, obituaries, advertisements, crossword

Radio and TV

- To listen to a radio programme, you *tune in* to the *station* (or *wavelength*) you want. When you watch TV, you choose the *channel* you want.
- Some types of TV programme and the people involved:

Programme	People
news	newsreader
documentary	presenter
sports programme	commentator
chat show	host, guests
soap (opera)	actors
comedy show	comedian

Note: Chat show is British English. In the USA it's called a *talk show*.

15 Recent events

Present perfect simple tense

- We use the Present perfect simple to talk about recent events. It is often used for *announcing news* of something that has happened recently:
  Sarah *has got* engaged.
  There *has been* a plane crash at Heathrow Airport.
- If we want to focus on *what has happened* rather than on *who* has done the action, we often use the passive:
  A thief *has been arrested* (by the police).
  A new motorway *has been built*.
  (For tables of active and passive forms, see Unit 7.)

Present perfect and past simple tenses

- We use the Present perfect when we are not interested in *when* things happened, but only in *the fact* that they have happened. If we mention *when* or *how*, we use the Past tense:
  Sarah *got* engaged at the weekend.
  A plane *crashed* at Heathrow Airport last night as it was coming in to land.
- In a single paragraph, it is common to use the Present perfect for *announcing* a piece of news, followed by the past tenses for *going into details*:
  There *has been* a plane crash at Heathrow Airport. The crash *took place* late last night as the plane *was coming* in to land. Five passengers *were killed* and …

Present perfect continuous tense

- We use the Present perfect continuous to talk about *recent activities*. It answers the question 'How have you been spending your time?':
  I've *been writing* letters.
  I *haven't been working* very hard.
- Like the Present perfect simple, this tense cannot be used with past time expressions, but we can use it with expressions such as *recently*, *this week*, *over the last few days*:
  I've been writing a lot of letters *recently*.
  I haven't been working very hard *this week*.
- Forms of the Present perfect continuous:

I've She's	been working hard.
Have you Has she	been working hard?

Present perfect continuous and simple tenses

- Present perfect continuous and simple tenses are often used together. We use the continuous form to talk about *activities*, and the simple form to talk about individual *actions*:
  I've *been getting* ready for my trip. I've *packed* my case, I've *collected* my tickets and I've *changed* some money.
  I've *been writing* an essay. I've *written* it in rough but I *haven't typed* it out yet.

16 Teaching and learning

School subjects

Subject	Typical activities
languages	learning vocabulary; doing exercises; practising; translating
literature	reading novels, poetry, plays; writing essays
maths	making calculations; using tables
science	doing experiments
geography	using maps
history	learning dates; learning about governments, wars, leaders
art	painting, drawing
music	playing musical instruments
sport	playing football; doing athletics

- You *go to* (or *attend*) school.
  You *study* or *do* school subjects (e.g. I never did French at school).
  You *take* or *sit* examinations (exams), and you either *pass* or *fail* them.

Skills

- *good at* + *-ing* or noun.

I'm	(very) good quite good not very good no good	at	football. French. speaking French. singing.

- We can also say:
  I'm a good singer.
  She isn't a very good dancer.
- I *know how to* dance the tango. (= I can do it.)
  I *don't know how to* read music. (= I can't do it.)
  I *learnt how to* ride a horse when I was a child.

Schools and universities

- British and American equivalents:

GB	USA
nursery school	
primary school	grade school
secondary school	junior high school high school
university	college

- Before you leave school, you take a *school-leaving examination*. This qualifies you to go to *university*, where you study for a *degree*. When you get your degree, you *graduate* from university. Someone who has graduated from university is called a *graduate*. Note the pronunciation difference:
  to *graduate* /ˈgrædjʊeɪt/
  a *graduate* /ˈgrædjʊət/.

17 Narration

Past perfect tense

- We use the Past perfect tense to *go back* from a point in the past to events that had happened *earlier*:
  I came home at 4 o'clock, but I was too late: my brother *had* already *left*.
  The woman opposite me looked very familiar; I was sure I'*d seen* her somewhere before.
- Active and passive forms:

I He	had(n't)	met them before.

The car	had(n't) been	serviced. stolen.

I had, he had, etc., are often shortened to *I'd, he'd.*

- Notice the relationship between *how things were* in the past and *what had happened* earlier:

Past state	Previous event
The light *was* off.	Someone *had switched* the light off.
He *was* abroad.	He'*d gone* abroad.
There *wasn't* any hot water.	All the hot water *had been used* up.

Reported speech and thought

- Often we report what people said or thought in the past using verbs such as *said, told, discovered* and *realised*. When we do this, what the person actually said or thought usually changes *one tense further back*:
  'I'*m* French,' he said.
  → He said he *was* French.
  'I'*ve been* here before,' I thought to myself.
  → I realised that I'*d been* there before.
  'I'*ll* meet you at six,' she told me.
  → She told me she'*d* (= *would*) meet me at six.
- Tense changes in reported speech and thought:

Actual words		Reported
does	→	did
is doing	→	was doing
will do	→	would do
did	→	had done
has done		

- *say* and *tell*
  say is not followed by an object; *tell* is followed by an indirect object:
  He *said* he was French. (*not* he said me)
  He *told me* he was French. (*not* he told he was)
- Common reporting verbs:
  SPEECH: say, tell, explain, point out, reply, deny.
  THOUGHT: realise, discover, know, think.
- In certain cases (e.g. when reporting general facts or very recent speech) no tense change is necessary:
  Our teacher told us that penguins *live* in Antarctica.
  He said he'*ll* be there by 10 o'clock tonight.

18 Breaking the law

Crimes and criminals

A *criminal* is someone who *commits* a *crime*.

Crimes		Criminals
Verb	Noun	
rob	robbery	robber
(burgle)	burglary	burglar
(steal)	theft	thief
murder	murder	murderer
kidnap	kidnapping	kidnapper
hijack	hijacking	hijacker
blackmail	blackmail	blackmailer
spy (on)	spying	spy
smuggle	smuggling	smuggler
(vandalise)	vandalism	vandal

- You *steal* money or other things from people:
  He *stole* $100 *from* his cousin.
  They broke into our house and *stole* our TV.
  You *rob* people or places:
  They stopped him in a dark street and *robbed* him (of all his money).
  They *robbed* the National Bank.
- A *burglar* breaks into homes or shops and steals money or goods.
  A general word for someone who steals is a *thief*. The crime is *theft*.

Punishments

- If you commit a minor offence (e.g. parking your car in the wrong place), you may have to *pay a fine* (= pay money).
  If you commit a more serious crime, you may *be sent to* (or *go to*) *prison*.
  In some countries, people are *sentenced to death* for serious crimes (e.g. murder).

Trials

- The accused person *goes on trial* or *is tried* or *appears in court*.
- The *judge* is in charge of the trial.
  The *jury* decides if the accused is *guilty*.
  The *prosecution* tries to prove that the accused is guilty.
  The *defence defends* the accused.
  Witnesses give *evidence*.
- At the end of the trial, the jury give their *verdict* (either *guilty* or *not guilty*).
  If the accused is guilty the judge passes *sentence* (= decides on a punishment).

19 Up to now

Present perfect tenses with for and since

- We use the Present perfect continuous to talk about the duration of activities that started in the past and are still going on now:
  I've *been travelling* for 3 days.
  He's *been doing* the same job for 40 years.
- Some verbs are not normally used in the continuous form. With these verbs, we use the Present perfect simple:
  I've *had* this bicycle since I was a child.
  They've *been* here since Saturday.
- *for* is used with periods of time:
  for a year, for two weeks, for ages
  since is used with points of time:
  since 1950, since last week, since my birthday
  since can also be followed by a clause with a Past simple verb:
  I've been writing to her *since we met on holiday*.
  I've loved horses (ever) *since I was a child*.

Origin and duration

- When we talk about activities or states continuing up to now, we can focus on when they *started* (*origin*) or on *how long* they've been going on (*duration*).
  ORIGIN: He *became* a teacher five years ago.
  DURATION: He's *been* a teacher for five years.
  ORIGIN: They *started* building the dam in July.
  DURATION: They've *been building* the dam since July.
  Some common pairs of 'origin' and 'duration' verbs:

become	be
buy/get	have
move to	live (in)
meet / get to know	know
learn (how to)	know (how to)
fall in love	be in love
die	be dead

How long ...? and How long ago ...?

- Questions with *How long ago ...?* ask about *origin*:
  How long ago *did* you *meet* each other?
  – A year ago. / Last Christmas.
- Questions with *How long ...?* ask about *duration*:
  How long *have* you *known* each other?
  – For a year. / Since last Christmas.

Negative duration

- To express negative duration (how long something *hasn't* happened for), use the Present perfect simple:
  I *haven't visited* them for years.
  I *haven't spoken* French since I was at school.
  (*not* ~~I haven't been speaking~~ ...)
- Other structures that express negative duration:
  – *The last time* I visited them *was* years ago.
     The last time I spoke French *was* at school.
  – *It's* years *since* I (*last*) *visited* them.
     It's three years *since* I (*last*) *spoke* French.

20 In your lifetime

Birth, marriage and death

Event		Ceremony
Noun	*Verb*	
birth	be born	
	give birth (to)	
marriage	get married marry	wedding
death	die	funeral

- Before a baby is born, its mother is *pregnant*, or *is expecting a baby*. Then she *gives birth* (or *has the baby*), either in hospital or at home. A *midwife* helps to deliver the baby.
- In Britain and the US, many parents *christen* (= give a name to) or *baptise* their babies in church.
- At a wedding, the two people getting married are the *bride* and *bridegroom*. A wedding can be a *religious* ceremony (e.g. in church) or a *civil* ceremony (at a registry office). After the wedding, friends and relatives are invited to a *reception*. Then the couple go away on a *honeymoon*.
- When someone dies, the body is usually put into a *coffin*. At the funeral, the body may be *cremated* (= burnt) or *buried* in a *cemetery* (or *graveyard*). The *grave* is marked with a *gravestone* or *headstone*. Close relatives of the dead person usually go into *mourning*.

Ages

Person	Stage of life
child	childhood
adolescent/teenager	adolescence
adult/grown-up	adulthood
middle-aged person	middle age
old/elderly person	old age

- an *adolescent* is someone who is *growing up* (between child and adult). A *teenager* is someone between 13 and 19.
- *adult*, *grown-up* and *adolescent* can be used as nouns or adjectives:
  He behaves like a grown-up.
  He behaves in a very grown-up way.
- *Elderly* is a polite way to refer to old people.
- Other ways of talking about age:
  She's *in her* (*early/mid/late*) *twenties*.
  She's a *seven-year-old* (child).

Age and the law

In most countries, there is a *legal age* for certain activities.
- Often this is a *minimum age*:
  You *can't* drive a car *until* you are 17.
  You *have to* be 18 before you *can* vote.
- Or it may be a *maximum* age:
  You *have to* retire *at the age of* 65.

21 Finding out

Information questions

- Questions with *What ...?*

What	*kind of* bread shall I buy?
	type of music does she like?
	make of fridge have they got?
	colour paper did you get?
	size shoes does he wear?
	flavour soup would you like?

- *kind*, *type* and *make* are followed by *of*. Other category words are followed directly by another noun.
- Other questions with *What ...?*:
  What happened to your finger?
  What did you do to your finger?
  What happened to my coat? (= Where is it?)
- Questions with *How ...?*:
  – *How much/many, How long, How far, How often*:
  How much do you weigh?
  How far is it to the beach (from here)?
  – *How + adjective*:
  How expensive are the tickets?

Indirect questions

I wonder	if they're here.
I don't know	where they are.
Do you know	where they are?

- Indirect questions have normal word order. Compare:
  DIRECT: *Does* she *live* here?
  INDIRECT: I wonder if she *lives* here.

Reported questions

- As in reported speech (see Unit 17), the verb in a reported question changes one tense further back:
  '*Are* you French?'
  → He asked if I *was* French.
  '*Have* you *been* here before?'
  → She asked him if he'*d been* there before.
- Like indirect questions, reported questions keep normal word order:
  He asked me *where I lived*. (*not* ~~where did I live~~)

Question tags

- We use question tags:
  – to check things when we're not quite sure:
    You don't eat beef, do you? (rising intonation)
  – to express an opinion or belief:
    It's cold in here, isn't it? (falling intonation)
- To form question tags, repeat the auxiliary verb:
  They'*re* coming tomorrow, *aren't* they?
  You *can* swim, *can't* you?
  With Present and Past simple sentences, use *do(n't)* or *did(n't)*:
  She works for IBM, *doesn't* she?

22 Speaking personally

Feelings

angry	embarrassed	jealous	upset
annoyed	excited	nervous	worried
depressed	frightened	relaxed	

- *annoyed* = slightly angry.
  nervous = slightly afraid of something that's going to happen (e.g. an exam, a visit to the dentist).
  upset = very unhappy about something that's happened (you feel like crying).
- All these adjectives are used with *feel*, *get* and *make*:
  I *feel/get* frightened if I'm alone at night.
  Being alone at night *makes* me frightened.
- Adjectives ending in *-ed* have three equivalent forms:
  It *frightens* me.
  I makes me (feel) *frightened*.
  I find it *frightening*.

Reporting verbs

Notice how we use these verbs to report conversations:
  'Come on, cheer up – don't be sad.'
  – I tried to *cheer* him *up*.
  'OK, don't get angry – calm down.'
  – I tried to *calm* her *down*.
  'I'm very sorry.'
  – I *apologised*.
  'Go on – have a drink.'
  – He tried to *persuade* me to have a drink.
  'No, I don't want one.'
  – I *refused* (to have one).
  'This food's terrible.'
  – She *complained* about the food.

Reactions

'*Normal*' adjectives:
- With these adjectives we can use *very* or *quite*:
  The film was *very* disappointing.
  I found the film *quite* amusing.

Positive	Negative
good	bad
interesting	boring
enjoyable	dull
amusing	disappointing
entertaining	
exciting	

'*Extreme*' adjectives:
- *Wonderful*, *brilliant* and *terrific* all mean 'very good'. *Awful*, *dreadful* and *terrible* all mean 'very bad'.

Positive	Negative
wonderful	awful
brilliant	dreadful
terrific	terrible
fascinating	

- Because these adjectives already have the sense of 'very', we can't use the word *very* with them. Instead we use *absolutely* for emphasis:
  The film was *absolutely* wonderful.
  I found the film *absolutely* terrible.
- We can use *really* with normal or extreme adjectives:

The film was *really*	interesting.
	fascinating.

23 The unreal past

'Unreal' conditionals

2nd conditionals

> If + past tense … would/wouldn't (do)

- We use the second conditional to imagine unreal things in the *present*:
  If I were rich, I'd give a lot of money to help poor people. (I'm not rich – I'm just imagining it.)
  She'd be happier if she had a more interesting job. (In fact she's *not* very happy and her job *isn't* very interesting.)
  (See also Unit 9.)

3rd conditionals

> If + past perfect tense … would/wouldn't have (done)

- We use the third conditional to imagine unreal things in the *past*:
  If I'*d known* you were alone, I *would have visited* you. (Unfortunately I *didn't* know, so I *didn't* visit you.)
  I *would have been* upset if they *hadn't invited* me to the party. (In fact they did invite me, so it was all right.)
- Notice that to form unreal conditionals, the verb moves *one tense back*. So to talk about the present, we use the *Past tense*; to talk about the past, we use the *Past perfect tense*.

Mixed conditionals

- We can mix second and third conditionals in one sentence. One part can refer to the present (second conditional) and one part to the past (third conditional):
  If you'*d remembered* to buy some petrol, we'*d be* home by now.
  (You *didn't* remember, so we'*re not* home now.)

Expressing regret

- *I wish* + Past perfect tense is used for regretting past actions:
  I wish I'*d gone* to university. (I didn't go, and I regret it.)
  I wish I *hadn't shouted* at him. (I shouted at him, and now I'm sorry.)
  (For the use of *I wish* to make wishes about the present and future, see Unit 9.)
- *should(n't) have* + past participle is used for expressing regret or criticising past actions:
  I *should have* gone to university.
  I *shouldn't have* shouted at him.
  You *should have* told me. (You didn't tell me – that was wrong.)
  They *shouldn't have* stayed up so late. (They stayed up too late – now they're tired.)

24 Life on Earth

Global issues

Issues	Causes and effects
Air pollution	Factories, power stations and cars pollute the air → acid rain → trees are damaged.
Pollution of the sea	Industrial waste and sewage is dumped in the sea → wildlife is killed.
Global warming	Gases from cars and power stations → 'greenhouse effect' → the Earth becomes warmer → the climate changes → sea level rises.
Destruction of the rain forest	Trees are cut down → species become extinct, increases 'greenhouse effect'.
Nuclear power	Nuclear accidents → radioactive material escapes into the atmosphere → causes cancer.
Ozone layer	Chemicals destroy the ozone layer → sun causes skin cancer, damages crops.
Desertification	Overuse of farmland → desert spreads → farmland is lost.

- Notice these verb/noun pairs:

Verb	Noun
destroy	destruction
pollute	pollution
damage	damage (to)
protect	protection

Environmental action: verbs

- To help the environment:
  – *save* electricity; don't *waste* it
  – don't *use* more electricity than you need
  – *recycle* glass and paper; don't *throw* it *away*.
- Governments can *increase* or *decrease* (*raise* or *lower*) the price of certain products.
  They can *tax* (or *put a tax on*) products or *ban* them (= make them illegal).
- These are all things that can be done to *protect* the environment.

Wildlife

- Animals, birds, fish and insects are forms of *wildlife*.
- Many animals that were once *common* have become *endangered species*: they are so *rare* that they could *become extinct*.
- Some animals are *hunted* for their meat or skins; others are in danger because their *habitat* is being destroyed.
- Many rare animals are *protected* by law (= it is illegal to kill them), and live in *wildlife reserves*; some also live *in captivity* (e.g. in zoos).

Verb forms

Verb tenses

Here is a summary of verb tenses taught in this book (numbers refer to units).

	Simple	*Continuous*
Present	go/goes (1)	am/is/are going (1)
Past	went (3, 7, 19)	was/were going (3)
Present Perfect	have/has gone (7, 15, 19)	have/has been going (15, 19)
Past Perfect	had gone (17, 23)	(had been going)
Future	will go (11)	will be going (11)
Future Perfect	will have gone (11)	(will have been going)
Conditional	would go (9)	(would be going)
Past Conditional	would have gone (23)	(would have been going)

The Passive

The passive is formed with *be* + past participle. It can be in any tense: past, present or future:

Present: Wheat *is grown* all over Europe.
Past: They *were rescued* by helicopter.
Present perfect: The house *has been sold.*
Past perfect: I noticed that the lights *had been left* on.
Future: The road *will be opened* in six months' time.

The passive also has a continuous form, but this is commonly used only in the Present and Past tenses:

Present: My flat *is being redecorated.*
Past: He *was being questioned* by the police.

Infinitives

The infinitive is the basic form of the verb. It is used after *to* and after modal verbs. There are four possible forms: present or past, simple or continuous:

	Simple	*Continuous*
Present	work	be working
Past	have worked	have been working

Examples:
Be quiet now – I want to *work.*
He's not at the office – he must *be working* at home today.
No wonder you failed the exam – you should *have worked* harder.
She's nearly 70, so she must *have been working* here for at least 50 years.

Common functions

Asking people to do things

– *Would you* pass the salt, please?
– *Could you* give me a lift to the station?
– *Would you mind* taki*ng* your shoes off?

Asking permission

– *Can I* take my shoes off?
– *Do you mind if I* turn the radio on?
– *Is it all right if I* bring a friend?

Making suggestions

– *Let's* go for a swim.
– *Why don't we* buy a CD player?
– *How about* (mak*ing*) a cup of coffee?

Giving advice

– *I think you should* go to bed earlier.
– *You'd better* tell the police immediately.
– *If I were you, I'd* complain about it.

Deciding and choosing

– *I think I'll* buy a newspaper.
– *I'd like* an orange juice, please.
– *I'd rather* stay at home and watch TV.

Making offers

– *Shall I* bring some food?
– *I'll* call a taxi *if you like.*
– *Would you like to* see my holiday photos?

Asking for information

– *Can you tell me* what time the film starts?
– *Do you know* where I can find a dictionary?
– *I wonder if you could tell me* the way to the station.

Irregular verbs

Infinitive	Simple past	Past participle
be	was/were	been
beat	beat	beaten
become	became	become
begin	began	begun
bend	bent	bent
bite	bit	bitten
blow	blew	blown
break	broke	broken
bring	brought	brought
burn	burnt	burnt
build	built	built
buy	bought	bought
can	could	(been able)
catch	caught	caught
choose	chose	chosen
come	came	come
cost	cost	cost
cut	cut	cut
do	did	done
draw	drew	drawn
dream	dreamt	dreamt
drink	drank	drunk
drive	drove	driven
eat	ate	eaten
fall	fell	fallen
feed	fed	fed
feel	felt	felt
fight	fought	fought
find	found	found
fly	flew	flown
forget	forgot	forgotten
forgive	forgave	forgiven
freeze	froze	frozen
get	got	got
give	gave	given
go	went	gone (been)
grow	grew	grown
hang	hung	hung
have	had	had
hear	heard	heard
hide	hid	hidden
hit	hit	hit
hold	held	held
hurt	hurt	hurt
keep	kept	kept
know	knew	known
lay	laid	laid
lead	led	led
learn	learnt	learnt
leave	left	left
lend	lent	lent
let	let	let
lie	lay	lain
lose	lost	lost
make	made	made
mean	meant	meant
meet	met	met
pay	paid	paid
put	put	put
read	read	read
ride	rode	ridden
ring	rang	rung
rise	rose	risen
run	ran	run
say	said	said
see	saw	seen
sell	sold	sold
send	sent	sent
set	set	set
shake	shook	shaken
shine	shone	shone
shoot	shot	shot
show	showed	shown
shut	shut	shut
sing	sang	sung
sink	sank	sunk
sit	sat	sat
sleep	slept	slept
smell	smelt	smelt
speak	spoke	spoken
spell	spelt	spelt
spend	spent	spent
spread	spread	spread
stand	stood	stood
steal	stole	stolen
sweep	swept	swept
swim	swam	swum
swing	swung	swung
take	took	taken
teach	taught	taught
tear	tore	torn
tell	told	told
think	thought	thought
throw	threw	thrown
understand	understood	understood
wake	woke	woken
wear	wore	worn
win	won	won
write	wrote	written

Phonetic symbols

Vowels

Symbol	Example
/iː/	tree /triː/
/i/	many /'meni/
/ɪ/	sit /sɪt/
/e/	bed /bed/
/æ/	back /bæk/
/ʌ/	sun /sʌn/
/ɑː/	car /kɑː/
/ɒ/	hot /hɒt/
/ɔː/	horse /hɔːs/
/ʊ/	full /fʊl/
/uː/	moon /muːn/
/ɜː/	girl /gɜːl/
/ə/	arrive /ə'raɪv/
	water /'wɔːtə/
/eɪ/	late /leɪt/
/aɪ/	time /taɪm/
/ɔɪ/	boy /bɔɪ/
/əʊ/	home /həʊm/
/aʊ/	out /aʊt/
/ɪə/	hear /hɪə/
/eə/	there /ðeə/
/ʊə/	pure /pjʊə/

Consonants

Symbol	Example
/p/	pull /pʊl/
/b/	bad /bæd/
/t/	take /teɪk/
/d/	dog /dɒg/
/k/	cat /kæt/
/g/	go /gəʊ/
/tʃ/	church /tʃɜːtʃ/
/dʒ/	age /eɪdʒ/
/f/	for /fɔː/
/v/	love /lʌv/
/θ/	thick /θɪk/
/ð/	this /ðɪs/
/s/	sit /sɪt/
/z/	zoo /zuː/
/ʃ/	shop /ʃɒp/
/ʒ/	leisure /'leʒə/
/h/	house /haʊs/
/m/	make /meɪk/
/n/	name /neɪm/
/ŋ/	bring /brɪŋ/
/l/	look /lʊk/
/r/	road /rəʊd/
/j/	young /jʌŋ/
/w/	wear /weə/

Stress

We show stress by a mark (/'/) before the stressed syllable:
later /'leɪtə/; arrive /ə'raɪv/; information /ɪnfə'meɪʃn/

Acknowledgements

The authors would like to thank the following for their contributions to *Language in Use* Intermediate:

– for contributing to the listening and reading material: Carlos Aradas-Balbás, Carolyn Becket, Mª Celina Bortolotto, Jake Bundy, Lucy Bundy, Deb Clark, Bryan Cruden, James Dingle, Maria Dingle, Kayoko Enomoto, Jahel Fabris, Amy Fisher, David Fisher, Colette Fitzpatrick, Véronique Foray, Genevieve Higgins, Laura Jerran, Sakae Katoh, Catriona Maclachlan, Jonathan Mullan, Sally Mullan, Mike Mendenhall, Alan Ogilvy, Shane Pope, Helen Sandiford, Ewa Simbieda, Aileen Smith, Carsten Williams, Ingrid Williams, Jan Williams, Larissa Williams, Tony Williams, Gabriela Zaharias; and all the actors whose voices were recorded in studio sessions.

– for the production of the recorded material: Martin Williamson (Prolingua Productions), Peter Taylor (Taylor Riley Productions Ltd.), and Peter and Diana Thompson (Studio AVP).

The authors would also like to thank the following at Cambridge University Press:

– Colin Hayes for his continuing support and help.
– Peter Donovan for organising and steering the project through its various stages.
– Nick Newton and Anne Colwell for organising and overseeing design and production.
– Joanne Currie for her excellent design.
– Catherine Boyce for her work on the Pilot edition.
– Molly Bannister, Sue Featherstone and Val Grove for general administrative help.
– James Dingle, our Editor, for his tireless dedication, constructive ideas and good judgement.

The authors and publishers would like to thank the following institutions and teachers for their help in testing the material and for the invaluable feedback which they provided:

A.C.T., Paris, France; Rowan Ferguson, Executive Language Services, Paris, France; Lanser SA, Paris, France; The British Council, Athens, Greece; John Eaglesham, British School, Milan, Italy; Centro Linguistico di Ateneo, Parma University, Parma, Italy; Ridge International, Osaka, Japan; Tessa Pacey, ILC, Tokyo, Japan; Sunshine College Tokyo, Japan; Janaka Williams, Simul Academy, Kyoto, Japan; Lexis, Granada, Spain; LinguaSec, Madrid, Spain; Joe Hogan, The House, Palafrugell, Spain; English 1, Seville, Spain; Istanbul Technical University, Istanbul, Turkey; Özel Eyüboğlu Lisesi, Istanbul, Turkey; Roger Scott, Bournemouth, UK.

The authors and publishers are grateful to the following copyright owners for permission to reproduce copyright material. Every endeavour has been made to contact copyright owners and apologies are expressed for any omissions.

pp. 30–1: Times Editions Pte Ltd for texts adapted from *Britain*, *Singapore*, *Spain* and *Thailand* in the *Culture Shock* series, published by Kuperard (London) Ltd; The Rough Guides for text adapted from *The Rough Guide to West Africa*; p. 38: advertisements and Yellow Pages cover reproduced by kind permission of BT Yellow Pages. 'Yellow Pages' is a registered trademark of British Telecommunications plc in the United Kingdom; pp. 40–1: GE Magazines for text adapted from 'HELP! nobody loves us!' from *Me*, 10 July, 1989; pp. 48–9: John Murray (Publishers) Ltd for pictures and text adapted from *Victorian Inventions* by Leonard de Vries, 1991; p. 50: Simon & Schuster, Inc. for text adapted from *The Great Reckoning*, © James Dale Davidson and Lord William Rees-Mogg, 1993; p. 57: *Daily Record* and *Daily Mail*, © *Daily Mail* / Solo, for adapted text; p. 64: *The Beano*, © D. C. Thomson & Co. Ltd., *Car Magazine*, *Hello!*, *Homes and Gardens* and *Reader's Digest* for permission to reproduce covers; p. 66: *The Times* for text adapted from 'Easy Listening' by Joanna Pitman from *The Times* 22 May,

1992, © Times Newspapers Ltd. 1992; pp. 74–5: Multimedia for text adapted from *Your Memory, A User's Guide* by Alan Baddeley, © Multimedia Books Limited, published in the UK by Pelican and USA by Prion; p. 81: *The Times* for text adapted from 'Passenger "stabbed attacker on Tube with swordstick"'from *The Times* 10 September, 1987, © Times Newspapers Ltd. 1992. The names have been changed to protect those involved in the case; pp. 82–3: MindTrap Games Inc. for texts adapted from the board game *MindTrap*, © MindTrap Games Inc.; p. 93: Leslie Thomas for *A Good Boy, Griffith* , © Leslie Thomas; p: 100: *The Observer* for text from 'The medicine' by Thomas Quirke, © *The Observer*; p. 101: Little, Brown and Co. (UK) Ltd. for text adapted from *Smile Therapy* by Liz Hodgkinson; pp. 108–9: *New Scientist* for adapted texts; p. 109: *The Times* for text adapted from 'August 14, 2116 – the End of the World?' by Nick Nuttal from *The Times* 26 October, 1992, © Times Newspapers Ltd. 1992.

The authors and publishers are grateful to the following illustrators and photographic sources:

Illustrators: Julie Anderson: pp. 51 *t*, 58, 71; Peter Byatt: pp. 13 *t*, 15, 17, 56, 66 *br*; Celia Chester: pp. 13 *b*, 92–3; Jerry Collins: pp. 55 *b*, 91 *b*, 118; Joanne Currie: p. 16 *t*; Richard Deverell: pp. 37, 94; Paul Dickinson: pp. 8, 65, 82–3; Lisa Hall: pp. 61 *b*, 66 *t*, 77 *b*; Sue Hillwood-Harris: p. 76; Phil Healey: pp. 74–5, 101; Frank Langford: pp. 16 *b*, 79; Angela Joliffe: pp. 64, 91 *t*; Vicky Lowe: pp. 66 *bl*, 78; Michael Ogden: pp. 11, 14, 88, 109 *t*; Amanda MacPhail: pp. 51 *b*, 55 *t*, 95, 117; Carl Melegari: p. 77 *t*; Nigel Paige: pp. 21, 84, 109 *b*; Bill Piggins: pp. 29, 42, 53, 61 *t*, 103 *t*, 113, 115, 119, 120; Tracy Rich: pp. 72, 103 *b*; Chris Ryley: p. 108; Jane Smith: pp. 23, 62; Sue Shields: p. 25; Kathy Ward: p. 98; Rosemary Woods: p. 43; Annabel Wright: pp. 10, 70, 81.

Photographic sources: Mohamed Ansar / Impact Photos: p. 90 *bl*; Apple Computer UK Ltd.: p. 36 *t*; Aqualisa for the focus spray from the Aqualisa Turbostream Power Shower System: p. 12 *bl*; Art Directors Photo Library: p. 24; Barnabys Picture Library: pp. 90 *br*, 117 *r*; The J. Allan Cash Photolibrary: pp. 90 *bc*, 117 *c*; Casio Electronics Ltd.: p. 36 *mc*; The Associated Press Ltd.: p. 65; Chinese and Japanese Special Fund, courtesy Museum of Fine Arts Boston for *Court Ladies Preparing Newly Woven Silk*: p. 34; Bruce Coleman Ltd.: pp. 107 *b*, 118; Colorific Photo Library: pp. 18, 73 *bl*, 117 *l*; Editions Minerva SA for pictures from *Life of the Aztecs in Ancient Mexico*, published by Productions Liber SA, 1978: p. 116; Mark Edwards / Still Pictures: p. 106 *m*; Greg Evans International: p. 68 *b*; Chris Fairclough Colour Library: p. 28 *bcr*; Mike Feeney / TRIP: p. 30; Sally and Richard Greenhill: pp. 31 *t*, 90 *ml*; Juliet Highet / TRIP: p. 90 *tl*; David Hoffman: p. 68 *tl*; The Hutchison Library: p. 106 *tl*; The Image Bank: p. 73 *br*; The Kobal Collection: p. 50; Peter Lake: pp. 12 *t*, *bc* & *br*, 20, 31 *b*, 39, 40–1, 44, 46, 54, 64, 81, 86 *br* (with thanks to Kate Dickens) & *bl*, 100, 104; Phil Loftus / Retna Pictures Ltd.: p. 66 *m*; Caroline Penn / Impact Photos: p. 90 *tcr*; Pictor International Ltd.: p. 86 *t*; Picturepoint-London: pp. 28 *bcl*, 66 *b*, 90 *mr*, 106 *tr*; Quadrant Picture Library: p. 52; Rex Features Ltd.: pp. 80, 106 *bl*; Helene Rogers / TRIP: pp. 31 *ml*, 86 *mr*; The Rolex Watch Company Ltd.: p. 86 *mcl*; Michael Rutland / Retna Pictures Ltd.: p. 86 *ml*; Sony United Kingdom Ltd.: p. 36 *mr*; South West News Service: p. 57; Tony Stone Images: pp. 9, 15, 28 *tl*, *bl* & *br*, 60, 73 *tl* & *m*, 106 *bc*, 107 *tl* & *tr*, 114, 120, 121; Sygma: p. 102; Syndication International: p. 66 *t*; Topham Picture Source: p. 86 *mcr*; Toshiba (UK) Ltd.: p. 36 *ml*; TROPIX / M. & V. Birley: p. 31 *mr*; TROPIX / M. Jory: p. 106 *tc*; Rob Turner / TRIP: p. 86 *bc*; Viewfinder Colour Photo Library: p. 29; Visionbank and England Scene: p. 68 *tr*; Zefa: pp. 28 *tr* & *m*, 73 *tr*, 90 *tcl* & *tr*, 107 *tc*, 112, 119.

t = top   *m* = middle   *b* = bottom   *r* = right   *c* = centre   *l* = left

Picture research by Sandie Huskinson-Rolfe of PHOTOSEEKERS.